How to Make Love to the Same Person for the Rest of Your Life*
*And still love it!

How to Make Love to the Same Person for the Rest of Your Life*
*And still love it!

DAGMAR O'CONNOR

Director, Sexual Therapy Program
Department of Psychiatry
St. Luke's–Roosevelt
Hospital Center, N.Y.

DOUBLEDAY & COMPANY, INC.
Garden City, New York
1985

Library of Congress Cataloging in Publication Data

O'Connor, Dagmar.
   How to make love to the same person for the rest of your
life, and still love it.

   1. Sex in marriage. 2. Sensuality. I. Title.
HQ21.O26   1985   646.7'8
ISBN 0-385-19854-X
Library of Congress Card Catalog Number 85–6869

For Gene, Ian, and Eric

Acknowledgments

This book could never have been written without the help of Daniel M. Klein who patiently listened to my thoughts, organized them, and helped me to put them on paper.

Above all, I want to thank William Masters, M.D., and Virginia Johnson of the Reproductive Biological Foundation in St. Louis for generously teaching me their innovative treatment techniques. As well, I am deeply indebted to all the couples who passed through my office over the years and taught me about the problems and joys of a committed relationship.

For professional support as mentors and co-therapists, I want to thank: The late Harley Shands, M.D., Director of Psychiatry, St. Luke's–Roosevelt Hospital Center; Stephen Katz, M.D., New York State Commissioner of Mental Health; Joseph Zubin, Ph.D., Lothar Gidro Frank, M.D., Stanley Coen, M.D., and Iona Ginsberg, M.D., all of Columbia University; Ellen Wachtell, Ph.D., and Stephen Reibel, M.D., both of St. Luke's–Roosevelt Hospital Center; and Martin Stone, M.D., of the State University of New York at Stony Brook.

For their generous help with this book a special thanks to: my legal advisor, Lawrence Gould; James Meltzer, Ph.D., and Alexander Elder, M.D., colleagues at St. Luke's–Roosevelt Hospital Center who read, criticized, and corrected with charity and enthusiasm; Birgitta and Stu Tray and Freke Vuijst for their critical readings; my agent, Mel Berger; my editor, Susan Schwartz; and my typists, Mary Ann Manfrini, Myrna Fleming, and Marceida Lopez.

Contents

Introduction

"How can I possibly make love to the same person for the rest of my life?"

After all the crazy things we've tried, all the barriers we've broken, who would have ever guessed that making vital, uninhibited love to the same person forever after would turn out to be the biggest sexual challenge of our lives?

But it is. And here is a book to answer that challenge.

How to Make Love to the Same Person for the Rest of Your Life is for those of us in the eighties who believe in sexual commitment again yet are terrified of sexual boredom. It is for all of us —single, married, divorced, or remarried—who have finally rejected one-night stands and serial affairs, secret infidelities and open marriages and who now yearn for one complete and lasting sexual relationship.

It is for the perplexed young woman who complained to me:

I graduated from the Sexual Revolution knowing everything there was to know about sex. I was a regular connoisseur of technique. The only thing I didn't learn was how to enjoy myself.

And it is for the perfectly healthy-looking middle-aged man who told me in utter sincerity:

Look, Phyllis and I have such a fulfilling relationship in every other way, it doesn't matter that we don't have much of a sex life anymore. It's a trade-off.

And it is for the millions of all ages who say:

I'd give anything to make our relationship last, but let's face it, promising to make love to only one person for the rest of my life is like promising to eat chicken salad every day for the rest of my life. The very words "committed sex" sound like life imprisonment.

Based on my fifteen years as a practicing Masters and Johnson–trained therapist, I have put together a book which I believe is much more than a survival handbook for the post–Sexual Revolution. It has a revolutionary premise of its own: *that lifelong committed sex has the potential to be more thrilling, more varied, more satisfying in every way than any other sexual arrangement you can think of.*

*   *   *

In recent years, more and more of the people I see in my practice function adequately—they can "do it" without any major problems—but they do not "do it" anywhere near as often as they would like to and they rarely "do it" with the gusto and pleasure they yearn for. As a result of working with a variety of couples—young and old, working class and professional, sexually conservative and sexually liberal—I developed techniques and exercises for dealing with the common problems of married sex life, for dealing with sexual infrequency and apathy, sexual monotony and numbness. I adapted some of these new techniques from Masters and Johnson exercises; others I developed and refined over the years in my Sexual Expansion Workshops for couples who wanted to make committed sex the best there is.

At the core of this book is original case material I gathered from the couples who attended these workshops. It shows how *every* couple can maximize their sexual potential. I examine the variety of ways modern couples turn themselves off to each other and how they can turn themselves back on in an evolving relationship. I explore the myths which have programmed us to turn off to experimental or frivolous sex in a "serious" relationship, The "Swept Away" Myth and The "Real Thing" Myth. I analyze how we have learned to numb ourselves to sexuality in families and how we can "UnMommy" our wives and "UnDaddy" our husbands to become true lovers again. I look at the ways that competitiveness, anger, jealousy, and fear of intimacy can rob sex of all its joy.

Then, in the second half of the book, I show how we can think and feel sexually again and how we can "use" each other sexually in the very best sense of the word. I detail a whole smorgasbord of pleasures, of sensual sets and settings which can keep the adventure and seduction and even a sense of illicitness in an ongoing sexual relationship.

Unlike other recent books, this one does *not* tell you how to make love to whomever you happen to be with that night; nor does it describe in academic jargon laboratory-proven techniques for overcoming sexual dysfunctions; nor does it demonstrate with surveys and charts how our sexual practices compare with those of the rest of the population. I have tried to write a book for normal, intelligent people who want to combine the best of both worlds: a committed relationship and marvelous sex . . . *with the same person.*

PART I
How We Turn
Ourselves Off

1
The Turnoffs
of Everyday Married Life

Marriage is a perfect arrangement for avoiding sex. It can provide more alibis, excuses, distractions, and tensions to keep us from enjoying each other sexually than any other scheme designed by Man.

Yet marriage is also the best possible arrangement for enjoying the most exciting and pleasurable sex there is. It provides more opportunities for sexual variety, experimentation, and development than any alternative way that men and women have for making sexual contact with each other.

This is not a paradox—it is a matter of fundamental choice. We can either use marriage in service of our sexual guilts and anxieties to turn ourselves off. Or we can use it to turn ourselves on.

After fifteen years of practicing sex-therapy counseling, I am convinced that it is not marriage itself which turns any of us off: *We turn ourselves off in marriage.*

But my experience as a therapist has also convinced me that we have the power to turn ourselves back on and enjoy the absolute best sex there is.

Stated this way, it sounds very simple. But, of course, it is quite the opposite. It is all too easy to turn ourselves off in marriage: The habits and routines which deaden us sexually seem to come naturally. In Part I of this book we will look into the major ways many of us manage to become bored in marriage and why we do so—the self-destructive sexual myths we accept uncritically, the dangerous sexual games we play with each other, and the tricks we play on ourselves for avoiding one of the greatest pleasures that life—and marriage—offers us.

"It's Not Me, Babe"

Over the years, I feel like I have become a connoisseur of sexual alibis. Practically every day someone tells me that "it's not my fault" that his or her sex life has become infrequent, dull, and unsatisfying. It is marriage, the person's partner, "nature," or hundreds of other "circumstances beyond my control" which are to blame. And at first, they seem to be right:

"How can sex stay spontaneous when it's always the same body, the same smell, the same old routine?" they ask me. "Sexual boredom is built into marriage."

Or:

"He just doesn't turn me on anymore; I simply no longer feel anything when he touches me."

Or:

"Her body has changed. What can I tell you? She doesn't look sexy to me anymore."

Or:

"It's nobody's fault really. It's just that the 'chemistry' is gone. There's nothing anybody can do about that."

Or:

"I'm too old for sex."

Or:

"I'm either too tired for sex or he is."

Or:

"We haven't got enough time for sex."

Or, simply:

"It just doesn't work anymore."

For all of these people, sex had "lost its magic." When they did have sex, it was only "to get it over with," to keep their partner pacified, or to keep up their "weekly average." They rarely did it simply for pleasure. In fact, they rarely did it at all.

How could they blame themselves for that?

Yet these were often the very same people who told me that married sex *had to be* "mature," not the frivolous, silly stuff which teenagers indulged in. Or they were people who told me that making love when you are married *should be* full of feeling —preferably an expression of lifelong love . . . *every time*. Or they were people who, consciously or unconsciously, thought that wild sex or experimental sex—in fact, anything other than sexual intercourse—was not proper behavior for Moms and Dads. And very often they were people who had married for the comfort and security it afforded them, yet they felt sexually smothered by too much intimacy. In short, in these and in countless other ways, they had *used marriage* to turn themselves off—to make playful and exciting sex virtually impossible. *And then they had blamed marriage for their sexual apathy.*

When we consider all the sexual guilt and anxiety many of us are burdened with, beginning in childhood, it is little wonder that we find ways to avoid responsibility for sex for the rest of our lives. Sex, we decide, is something which "happens to us," not something which we make happen. This attitude makes its most obvious appearance in young women laden with guilt who will only indulge in sex when they are "swept away," when some "sexy devil" makes them lose their head. "It just happened—I couldn't help it," they tell themselves (and possibly their mothers) afterward. In fact, this is the way many young women end up with unwanted pregnancies: To have come *prepared* for sex with contraception would have made the act too conscious—and hence too guilt-ridden. To be "swept away" by sex makes us not responsible for it. *It just happens.* Men are not immune to this attitude either: Many justify their infidelities as the "frenzy of the moment." "I was carried away—I didn't know what was happening," they tell themselves (and possibly their wives) afterward. When sex "just happens" we do not have to feel guilty or anxious about it.

But sex rarely "just happens" in marriage. In fact, once we take our wedding vows—to make love to the same person for the rest of our lives—sex is suddenly something which *should happen.* And we should *make it happen.* Climbing into the marriage bed night after night, we find it difficult to make ourselves believe that sex is an "accident," that we are just "swept away in the frenzy of the moment." In marriage over the years, it becomes virtually impossible to avoid making sex a *conscious act.* And that is both its burden and its potential joy. Because conscious sex can be fraught with anxieties. But conscious sex can also be the best sex there is.

Sadly, sexual anxieties become magnified for many once marriage begins. Sex is too much *there,* too conscious a possibility for many of us to manage, and so, instead of dealing with these anxieties, we devise ways to avoid sex in marriage altogether— or at least to avoid exciting sex. Now, instead of sex "just happening," *"it just does not happen." We* are not responsible for our sexual infrequency or apathy. The "chemistry" is gone; we are not "swept away" anymore; we are too "busy" for sex. *It is not our fault.*

But it is.

You Turn Yourself on . . . and Off

We are potentially sexual all of the time. Sex is there ready and waiting for us to express it every moment of the day. We can become aroused by a fleeting fantasy in the laundry room, a passage in a book, a photo in a magazine, a stranger's thigh accidentally brushing against our own on a commuter train, the brief glimpse of a young woman walking by the window. Yet we routinely—and automatically—turn ourselves off before these stimuli can affect us.

As Freud stated in *The Psychopathology of Everyday Life,* the repression and suppression of our sexuality is what makes Man civilized. Without these safeguards we would be sexually active helter-skelter with just about everyone—love would vanish, the family would disappear, work would go undone. But most of us, alas, become *overcivilized.* Heaven forbid that we allow ourselves to become aroused by the fleeting brush of that stranger's thigh or by a sexual fantasy at work. We go through our days in a perpetual state of sexual numbness out of fear of being inappropriately turned on. By the time we make contact with our partner again at home, we have been turning ourselves off all day. And that is only the beginning. Because Home is the ultimate turnoff.

The Unsexiest Place in the World—Home

Compared to home, the rest of the world is a potential orgy. Most of us feel more aroused by our fleeting fantasies about some of our co-workers than we feel when we walk in the door and peck our husband or wife on the cheek. Home is the scene of our greatest anxieties, our major responsibilities, and our most upsetting conflicts. It immediately sets us thinking about bills to be paid and duties to be performed, children to be taken care of and arguments to finish, schedules, routines . . . just about everything but sex. And on top of it all, home is the place where we are a family, just like we were with Mom and Dad— This fact alone can reactivate all the automatic turnoffs we learned as children in our first families. True, Home is also the source of our greatest solace and comfort, our shelter against the storm of the world's dangers and madness but, as we will see later, this also contributes to making Home a very unexciting place. No, Home is about the unsexiest place in the world. It is also the place where we have committed ourselves to making love to just one person for the rest of our lives.

"Who can feel sexy while the washing machine is running?" one woman said to me. "Or when you know people are coming for dinner in an hour? Who can respond to a passionate kiss in the kitchen when the kids might walk in? And who can swing from the chandelier and growl like a tiger when the kids are in the next room doing their homework? I've given up on sex at home. It's simply the wrong place for it."

Specifically, the "wrong place for sex" is our bedrooms, the most anxiety-laden spot in the house. The bedroom is the place where we have our biggest fights and arguments because it is the only private place where the children will not hear us. It is the place where we negotiate who will get up first and it is the place where we battle over blankets and space, about snoring and night-lights. It is the place where we sleep. And this is the *one* place where we are allowed to turn on sexually for the first time all day. "It's eleven o'clock, time to turn on." But how?

Turning ourselves on requires relaxedly focusing on our sexual feelings and shutting everything else—all the distractions and anxieties—out. We cannot expect to learn how to do this in a day or a week or even a month. It is a question of refocusing our whole lives until our sexual feelings become one of the most important parts of our lives again.

Probably the easiest way we can start to convince ourselves that we are in charge of what we feel is by a simple, sensate exercise which demonstrates how much control we have over our sensual responses:

> Caress the back of your arm with your hand while focusing on a specific problem which is bothering you—say, money or the children. Or simply do the same in the midst of home distractions—kids screaming, washing machine chugging.
>
> Now, find yourself a quiet spot where you will not be interrupted and again caress the back of your arm. Close your eyes, relax as much as you can, let your fantasies wander, and focus on your feelings.
>
> Examine the difference. In the first instance, you probably felt very little; in the second, you probably felt much more. The "touch" was not different, only the way in which you allowed yourself to experience it.

Daring to Feel Good

Marriage truly is the best possible arrangement for enjoying the most exciting sex there is. That is because we must *will* sex in marriage—we must consciously decide that sex is what we want to make happen—and so we can consciously experiment and develop with each other in a spirit of both trust and adventure. *We* are in charge of our sex lives now—not "magic" or "chemistry." We can feel anything we want to.

And the best way to start is by trying sexual exercises and games together. Over the years, I have adapted Masters and

Johnson exercises for those of us who do not have sexual dysfunctions, but who have simply lost their sexual verve and vigor and sense of adventure. As well, along the way I have designed several exercises and games of my own to help us recontact the sexual feelings we have covered up and to rediscover each other's bodies. The exercises are simple and progressive: They start with taking turns just touching one another and move, by steps, to all kinds of sexual adventures. No matter how far along you feel you are already, I am convinced that it is best to start at the beginning with Touching Exercise I; if nothing else, it helps you get used to the idea of setting aside a special time to consciously experiment with sex—that, in itself, is the biggest hurdle for most of us to overcome.

Whenever I give an exercise to a couple, someone always groans:

"Sex is supposed to be spontaneous. It will take all the joy out of it to make it an exercise like calisthenics. It sounds too much like work."

Or:

"We're not children. These sound like children's games."

Or:

"We don't have the time."

Each of these is, I believe, a resistance to making sex conscious—an act of will. It makes us anxious to confront both our desires and our fears so deliberately. I do not believe for a minute that these exercises make our sex less spontaneous in any basic sense: Our sexual responses are always spontaneous; we are only creating relaxed and inviting circumstances in which these spontaneous responses can happen. And yes, these exercises are as playful as children's games—thank goodness. Their major purposes are to help us overcome the seriousness with which we approach "mature" married sex and to transport us back to our earliest sensual experiences. We are quite capable of having "immature" sex without making it irresponsible sex. And finally, if we do not have the "time" for these exercises, then we have already decided that we do not have the time for sex—that it is our lowest priority. Before you even begin you have to decide *together* that sex might be at least as important as watching television or going to your aerobic dance class or having dinner with friends; the time is there if sex is important enough to you.

Yet with all of this said, I still know very well how hard it is to begin trying these exercises: They make us feel self-conscious and silly or, worse, they make us feel as if we must be a "case" if we have to resort to such contrived means to make our sex lives better. I can only assure you that the hardest part is simply beginning—taking a leap of faith, daring to feel good—because from the moment you begin, pleasure begins. The exercises are not meant to be hard work, they are meant to be playful fun. Try them in the same spirit you would try a new kind of food or a new place for a holiday. It is an adventure. And you will begin to feel the results of this adventure very soon: You can recontact sensual feelings and responses that may have lain dormant for years; you can relearn how to relax and take pleasure without the guilt of feeling selfish or self-indulgent; you can begin again to see each other's bodies as a source of marvelous sensual and sexual pleasure. In short, these exercises can help you stop turning yourself off and start turning yourself on again.

2
"I'm in the Mood for Love. . . . Why Aren't You?"

There is a scene in the Woody Allen film *Annie Hall* which everyone seems to remember. The screen is split: On one side Woody is in his psychiatrist's office; on the other his lover (Diane Keaton) is in *her* psychiatrist's office. Both are being asked how often they make love.

"Hardly ever," Woody answers. "Maybe three times a week."

"Constantly," Diane answers. "I'd say three times a week."

It is no accident people remember this scene: It strikes home. In just about every marriage there is some sexual imbalance: One partner wants to make love more frequently than the other. And both complain that they are rarely in the mood for sex at the same time.

"That's why marriage can never work," one recently separated man said to me. "It's preposterous to think that two people will want to make love at the same time with any regularity. It's about as likely as dealing the same poker hand twice on one night—the odds are simply against it. And all those times when one of you is in the mood and the other isn't, you're just stuck—you can't make love to anybody else."

"Wasn't there anything else you and your wife did at the same time regularly?" I asked him. "Not even have dinner together?"

"Having sex and having dinner are hardly the same," the man replied. "You don't have to be in the right mood to have dinner."

"Sure you do," I said. "But you have no problem getting your stomach into the right 'mood' when the food arrives at six o'clock every night. And I think the same can be true of sex—you can get yourself in the mood by the time the main course arrives—*if you are willing to."*

"Easier said than done," the man said.

Indeed it is.

The Princess and the Pill

A great many men and women wait for the "perfect mood" to strike before they engage in sex, the same way that a romantic poet waits for the perfect inspiration before he begins to write.

"Sex is not a mere physical thing, like an itch or going to the bathroom," one woman, Gwynne G., said to me. "It's a totally magical feeling that just comes over me. I can't plan it. And if Jack tries to create the mood—you know, candlelight and champagne—I usually get totally turned off. He's just so deliberate and obvious about it. *I can't help myself."*

Here once more is our old friend "I can't help myself." It is the catchall phrase which allows us to avoid sex as much as possible without ever having to take any responsibility for it. And believe me, people who wait for the perfect "inspiration" to have sex rarely have sex at all. Like Gwynne, they often will not even allow themselves to be gotten into the mood; their partners' attempts are "too deliberate and obvious." In other words, it makes sex too conscious.

Unfortunately, Gwynne was married to a man who needed sex on a regular basis. Jack told me that if he did not have sex at least once a week, he became terribly anxious and grumpy.

"If I go too long without sex, I can't sleep," he said. "It's like a vitamin pill I need to take regularly or I just go bananas. But if I say anything like that to Gwynne, she gets furious. She says that she doesn't want to be a vitamin pill, she wants to be a princess. We're just badly matched, I'm afraid."

True, Jack and Gwynne seemed badly sexually matched—at least by the time they came to see me. But as I quickly realized, they had not always been that way. Over the years they had *polarized* one another. Yes, Gwynne had always wanted to be "in the mood" before she had sex, but at the beginning of her relationship with Jack she had been "inspired" two and three times a week. Likewise, Jack had always had a steady need for sex but it had been perfectly satisfied at the beginning. Yet as time went on, Gwynne began to see Jack's "need" as a drag on her; she felt blackmailed by his threats of glum moods, so she retreated more and more into her position of "waiting for the magical moment when I would be turned on." And Jack began to feel more and more rejected: No matter how hard he tried to create the "magic" for his wife, she was rarely interested anymore. And the more rejected Jack felt, the greater his need became—not just his physical need, but his emotional need to feel connected to Gwynne, to be reassured that she still cared for him. Jack and Gwynne were stuck. The space between them had become wider. They had pushed one another to extremes.

Like many women—and men too—Gwynne resented simply being "used" to fulfill her husband's needs. She felt it cheapened her, cheapened their relationship, and cheapened sex itself. Another woman I know says her husband always refers to sex as his "Geritol," and another said her husband calls sex his "itch." It is enough to make anyone yearn for at least a little bit of romance.

On the other hand, it would be a silly distortion to imagine that sex was not a continuing natural need, both physical and emotional. Life without some regularity of sex and physical communication—especially married life—can be very dismal. At the most basic level, we are all still little children who need to be stroked or we will become despondent. "Need" is not a dirty word; it describes the sexuality of *all* of us, even if we are loath to admit it. As I said to Gwynne, "Stop worrying about Jack's sexual needs and start trying to feel your own."

Still, seeing sex as simply another of our animal needs on a par with food, drink, and going to the bathroom can make it very unappetizing. Men, especially, who view sex this way tend to reduce it to a mechanical—and purely genital—act totally devoid of feeling and personal contact. They tend to want to "get down to business." Touching and affection are simply means to an end—"priming the pump," so to speak—so that the "need" can be taken care of. These husbands may be dutiful "Hard Workers" who methodically go about getting their wives "ready," but their wives do not need to be psychologists to sense that something is missing—that getting to orgasm is the sole purpose of all this warming up.

"I always try to do at least fifteen minutes of foreplay," Jack told me earnestly. "It's not like I pounce on her."

" 'Foreplay' is the most unsexy word I know," I answered. "It's a dead giveaway that it's just something you have to get out of the way before you get down to what you're really after."

Jack was not focused on the process of lovemaking, on all the pleasures which merely touching and being touched could afford both of them: No, he only was focused on the end. Little wonder that Gwynne was constantly waiting for the perfect mood, and blaming him that it never arrived.

Time and again, I see women who complain of "end-oriented" husbands.

"He knows all the right buttons to push," one woman said to me. "He's got it down to a science. Five minutes on my breasts, then—bingo!—he dives for my clitoris and puts in ten minutes there before he climbs on top of me. I feel like a pinball machine."

This woman went on to say that she usually did get turned on and have an orgasm, "but there was something so one, two, three about it that began to wear on me. After a while I was spending more time fantasizing about having a romantic lover and less time in bed having mechanical orgasms with my husband."

All the women I see, no matter how uninhibited they have become sexually, still crave touching and affection for its own sake—not just as a warm-up. At the risk of being labeled sexist, I have to report this fundamental difference in male and female sexuality which I see again and again: Women, no matter how readily orgasmic they are, are less likely than men to become purely end-oriented. No doubt it all starts in childhood; studies show that young girls generally receive much more physical affection than young boys and so the pattern—and the differences—begin. By the time these boys and girls reach adulthood, the makings of a male/female sexual mismatch is often there.

Like Gwynne and Jack, they can become polarized: One, yearning for affection, endlessly waits for a "magic moment"; the other, needing to "get down to business," constantly lives with his own frustration.

The first "assignment" I gave Gwynne and Jack was a simple paradoxical exercise designed to depolarize them. I asked them to make a deal with one another:

For one month, Gwynne was to allow Jack to ask for sex as often as once a day. And when he asked, Gwynne had to respond by physically initiating sex.

At first, Gwynne resisted, but finally she said, "I'll do it, but I'm not promising I'll like it—or him."

"That's okay," I said. "Don't enjoy it any more than you want to."

As so often happens, Jack asked to make love every day for the first week, once every other day the second week, and by the third and fourth week he was content with twice a week. Typically, Gwynne had assumed that he would want "it" all the time; but he had only wanted sex all the time when it seemed that he could not have it at all. Furthermore, Gwynne timidly admitted that by about the third week she found that she enjoyed their sex "a little more" than she had expected, that once they got started she "somehow got into the mood." I had hoped for this response. Many men and women have told me that it is the "getting started" which is their problem; once things "get rolling" they have no trouble responding.

Once they were able to stop seeing one another in extremes —"Me as a sex maniac and her as a nun," as Jack put it— Gwynne and Jack were ready to take the next step toward a mutually enjoyable sex life. My next assignment for them was Touching Exercise #1—to have sex that did not lead to orgasm at all.

Touching Exercise #1

Take turns touching and being touched.

Decide who will be the toucher first and who will be the touchee.

Nude in your bedroom with the door locked and the light on (and the phone off the hook), let your partner touch you all over—except on the breasts and genitals. Do not allow yourself to touch your partner back. You have only one responsibility: to communicate to your partner if anything he or she does is unpleasant. This keeps you in charge and your partner knowing that he or she is only giving you pleasure.

Try to communicate nonverbally. For example, put your hand over your partner's hand—move your partner's hand away if something does not feel good or if you are ticklish in a particular area.

Close your eyes: You are now free to focus on your sensations, not on your partner. You do *not* have to interpret the expression on his or her face or to wonder what he or she is feeling. *This is for you.*

Try not to expect anything: Just feel what you feel. The first time you try this exercise, you may feel anxious, your mind may wander, you may even feel nothing at all and start wondering why you are not getting turned on. Try to ignore these thoughts and feelings and to keep coming back to just your sensations.

Do not feel obligated to give your partner positive feedback —to say "that feels good" or to moan. If these responses come spontaneously, fine and good. If not, do not distract yourself from your sensations with them.

Let the experience go on for a minimum of fifteen minutes and a maximum of forty-five. Do not look at the clock: You have one in your head. The touchee decides when the experience is over. Do not try to interpret when your partner has "had enough" or if he or she is bored. Again, the experience is for you. You do not have to give your partner equal time.

The toucher may indeed feel bored or awkward or even hurt and rejected if he or she does not get enough feedback or if you become so relaxed you fall asleep. But the toucher should try to ignore these feelings and get on with the pleasure of giving pleasure. And to remember that later on in the evening it's his or her turn to be the touchee.

Finally, do not cheat and use the touching exercise as foreplay to intercourse. Just experience the arousal itself. You can go one evening without orgasm—it won't make you ill. You can enjoy the appetizer without having to eat the whole meal.

The main idea of this exercise was, of course, to allow Jack to become acquainted in a leisurely fashion with his own sensual feelings—feelings which he had previously only experienced in service to his ultimate goal, orgasm. He was forced to lie back and passively feel these sensations for their own sake; he could relax with them. Also, when Jack took his turn touching Gwynne, he learned to take the "fore" out of "foreplay." It was purposely not leading anywhere, so he was able to discover the pleasure of touching her for its own sake. And of watching her take pleasure in it too.

But this exercise—and those touching exercises which followed—were not only for Jack's benefit. By touching and being touched regularly, Gwynne was able to come to terms with her own sexual needs. She had them too. All those years when she had spent most of her time "waiting for the magical moment," she had been thwarting her own needs—not just Jack's. And once she "got started," the mood was there.

"I'd been waiting for the right mood," Gwynne said happily at our last session, "but the fact is the mood was waiting for me."

"Hey, That Was Terrific—Why Don't We Do This More Often?"

"Getting started" is the biggest hurdle in most marriages, the largest single cause of that scourge of married life, sexual infrequency. Once a couple has made the decision to have sex that evening (or morning or afternoon) *and* the act is begun—one button unbuttoned, one zipper unzipped—nothing much can stop it. But somehow most of us simply do not get started—at least not anywhere near as frequently as we want to. And if we don't start, nothing follows. As King Lear said, "Nothing will come of nothing."

"It's sheer madness," one man said to me. "I know that once we begin I'm going to love it. It's like jumping into the pool: Getting off the diving board is the hard part. Once I'm in, splashing around, I have a ball. But somehow there is always some reason why my wife and I never just begin."

And a woman who had come with her husband to see me because they made love infrequently said this: "It's strange, but whenever we *do* make love, we always look at each other afterwards and say, 'Hey, that was terrific. Why don't we do this more often?'"

Why don't they?

I suspect that the main reason most of us do not "jump right in" is that initiating sex has to be a *conscious decision* in marriage—it cannot be a "sudden inspiration" every time, week-in and week-out, not forever after. And along with this conscious decision come all the anxieties we have about sex. These anxieties cannot be "swept away," along with us, in the thrill of the moment. The fact is, we usually are not feeling all that sexy at the moment we make the decision to have sex—we are simply *planning on feeling sexy.* But without sexy feelings to ease the way, we have to coldly confront the basic implication of our decision: *We actively want the pleasure of sex.*

Simply admitting this to ourselves calls up an array of sexual fears and guilts which we do not have to confront when sex is more "inspirational." If, like many of us, you carry around the seemingly eternal guilt that sex is "dirty" and "bad" and that somehow you will be punished for enjoying it, you have to face this antisexual demon head-on every time you make the *conscious decision* to leap off the diving board and into the sack. But chances are you will change your mind before you jump.

Thus, when we think of initiating sex—or when our partner hints at it—we may decide, say, that it is too late in the evening to get started: We're too tired; we're afraid we'll get too little sleep. Or perhaps we decide it is *too early* to get started: Why go through all the bother of getting undressed and into bed when we will only have to get dressed again later? (Never mind that we think nothing of undressing and dressing for a game of tennis or a midday shower.) Or perhaps we schedule ourselves out of sexual opportunities with social engagements or work demands: We cannot have sex tonight because we "have to" go to the theater or finish a report. We even manage to avoid sex because of television: We "have to" catch the Late News before we go to bed and then it is "too late" for sex. In one Midwestern town which voluntarily gave up television for a month, the most notable result was that sexual frequency increased dramatically. It was not so much that without TV there was "nothing else to do"; rather, without TV, the last alibi for avoiding sex was removed.

The Sexual Seesaw and Other Dangerous Games

But "getting started" is only half the problem in most marriages. "Who starts" is the other half. The question of which partner initiates sex opens a Pandora's box of resentments, recriminations, and sexual power plays.

Brenda and Louis V., a Midwestern couple in their early forties, came to New York on their vacation for two weeks of intensive therapy. After fifteen years of marriage, their sex life had come to a full stop. Briefly, this is how they described what had happened: For their first fourteen years together, Louis had always been the one to initiate sex and nine times out of ten, Brenda had willingly acceded. But one evening, after a party at which Brenda had taken a few unaccustomed drinks, she reached over under the bedcovers and began to caress her husband's belly and thighs.

"He just pushed my hand away," Brenda said, still recalling the incident with obvious pain and resentment. "He told me I was drunk and he did not want to make love to me if I was going to act like that."

"I don't know why we have to keep going over this one night all the time," Louis cut in. "I've told you that I simply wasn't in the mood. And, damn it, you *didn't* seem like yourself that night. It would have been like making love to someone else." "Do you mean it wasn't like Brenda to touch you first?" I asked. "That is only part of it," Louis insisted. "The whole way she was acting—giggling and everything—wasn't like her."

For Louis, a giggling, sexually aggressive wife was not a wife at all: She was a hussy. And one does not make love to a hussy *in the marriage bed.* He was stuck with the classic male confusion: Women are either "madonnas" or "whores" and no man wants a whore as his wife and the mother of his children. For some men, this confusion leads to rarely having sex with their wives at all—sex is reserved for "whores," not "madonnas." For other men like Louis, as long as their wives acted like madonnas, they would make love to them; but the minute the wives gave signs of being "whores"—the minute they playfully initiated sex— the men turned themselves off. Louis insisted that she was "someone else"; otherwise, he would have to think that he had married a hussy.

But Brenda was angry, and the anger stayed with her. She realized that after all those years this had been the very first time she had initiated sex with her husband—and he had refused her. It was not her inhibitions alone which had kept her sexuality locked in—her husband wanted it locked in. Worse, he had made her feel guilty and ashamed of herself. He had made her feel cheap. Without fully realizing why she was doing it, Brenda began to pay him back. The next time Louis initiated sex, she begged off, saying that she was not in the mood. This was not merely spite; she really did not feel sexual. She refused the next time too, and the next. Louis, humiliated, stopped initiating sex altogether. They had not made love in a year.

Brenda and Louis offer an example of that most dangerous of marital games, the "Sexual Seesaw." In this game, it is not merely "bad timing" when one wants sex and the other does not. On the Sexual Seesaw, one partner does not want sex *because* the other does. Scores are being settled, sexual slights are being paid back: One sexual refusal deserves another, and up and down we go, never—or rarely—wanting sex at the same time. This game can last a week or a month or, with short periods of harmony in between, it can last an entire marriage. For Brenda and Louis, one up-and-down and the seesaw—and their sex life—came a halt.

Critical to whether we get onto the Sexual Seesaw is the way we respond to sexual refusal: If our partner refuses us two nights in a row, do we see that as a personal sexual rejection? Three nights? Four? Is a week of our partner's "headaches" enough to make us feel humiliated and angry—even if we know that our partner has been under pressure at work or in a generally depressed mood? Once we feel truly humiliated by a refusal, we usually respond by either stopping initiating sex—not risking another humiliation—or by paying back our partner by refusing him or her the next time he or she initiates sex. With that, the seesaw has begun.

Like a children's fight, it can escalate. Refusing sex becomes a power play: "If you say 'No,' so can I." The smallest unintentional sexual slight can seesaw its way up to total sexual war, particularly if one or both partners are sexually insecure. In the case of one unfortunate couple I saw, the wife actually did suffer from frequent migraine headaches—headaches so painful that making love during one could only exacerbate the pain and certainly be no pleasure. But her husband, who had always been unsure of himself sexually, ultimately saw these headaches as excuses—a sign that she did not find him sexually attractive anymore. His wife, trying to make things up to him, initiated sex with him when she was feeling well, but finally it was too late for him: He was stuck in his humiliation and defensiveness. He saw her sexual overtures as "patronizing" and would not respond; then *she* became angry and refused to respond to him next time. From a week of real headaches, they had seesawed themselves to a sexual stalemate.

It takes a certain amount of sexual security as well as generosity of spirit not to end up in one of these unhappy sexual cycles. A man who is easily humiliated on his job will all too easily see a sexual slight in his wife's reluctance to have sex one night, whatever her stated reason; and a woman who is convinced she is losing her attractiveness because of some added weight will interpret a week without sex as a sign that her husband has lost *all* sexual interest in her. From humiliation it is just one step to anger; and from anger the next step is all too frequently a payback.

When couples come to see me, often my first task is to point out how the cycle got started and to make the very simple observation that sometimes our partners *really are not in the mood for sex,* that every sexual refusal does not have to be seen as a sexual rejection. A partner who is under duress at work, who is tired or depressed, will probably not be in the mood for sex for a while and this has nothing whatsoever to do with us. Somehow, we are more willing to see a roommate's or friend's bad mood as just that—*their* problem, something which will pass. But when it comes to our sexual partners, we see a bad mood as our personal rejection: If he does not want to make love tonight, that means he is tired of me, cold, sexually bored; surely, it is the beginning of the end. It could not possibly be because he simply is not in the mood for sex *tonight.* I see countless men and women who never initiate sex with their partners anymore because they cannot risk a refusal—it is always seen as total rejection. And all it took was one refusal to confirm this for them.

Initiation Rights

But let us get back to Louis and Brenda. Their seesaw began with an incident considerably more loaded than just a passing mood: It crystallized an unspoken imbalance in their entire fifteen-year relationship. When Louis pushed Brenda's hand away, he was very clearly saying to her, "That is against the rules. Only I initiate sex between us. You have no initiation rights."

As we saw before, Brenda's transgression of this unspoken rule instantly turned her from a proper wife into a "wanton woman." It also instantly turned sex into a *demand* upon Louis: By reaching over to him under the covers, she was demanding that he perform sexually—at least that is the way he saw it—and he was overcome with anxiety. What if he was not up to the job? (And, of course, feeling so anxious he probably wasn't.) By al-

ways being the one to initiate sex, Louis had always been in
control and by being in control, he never had to experience sex
as a demand. But that night, he was threatened to the core.

That same night, Brenda had a revelation: She had never had
sex with her husband simply because *she* wanted it. She had
always waited for him to initiate it. Perhaps she had hinted at
her desire with a look or gesture or a dab of perfume, but never
before had she taken direct action to get what she wanted. It
took a couple of drinks to finally get her to do this and when she
did, she was rebuffed. She got Louis's message loud and clear:
"Stay in your place! I'm the one who decides when we have
sex." And that message uncovered a resentment Brenda had
been carrying around inside her for fifteen years: *It wasn't fair.*
It took several sessions before Brenda was able to articulate this.

"It's not like I'm one of these modern women who wants her
own career and separate vacations and all that," Brenda said.
"But I have feelings too—sexual feelings. Why does it always
have to be on his terms? Why do I always have to wait for him to
be in the mood first?"

Brenda might have been speaking for better than half the
married women in America. Even in the most "liberated" marriages, where women do have careers, where household duties
and child care are shared equally, back in the bedroom they
rarely have "initiation rights." If the *husband* wants sex, he
reaches for his wife's body; if *she* wants sex, she reaches for the
perfume. And, as Brenda realized that night, it is not fair.

But I am not in the business of taking moral stands. If, say, I
were practicing sex therapy in Timbuktu (I somehow doubt
that there is even one sex therapist in all of Mali), I would not fly
in the face of tradition and insist that all women demand initiation rights. But Brenda was a rather typical American woman,
"modern" or not; and she felt cheated by the imbalance of the
sexual arrangement in her marriage. For fifteen years it had
only been an undercurrent of resentment; now it was open war.
My job was not to convince Louis of his "moral obligations" to
sexual fairness. It was to help them both rekindle their sexual
relationship and, ultimately, save their marriage.

I started by trying to show Brenda that all along she had been a willing accomplice in this sexual imbalance. It was not simply Louis's fault.

"I wonder what was in this arrangement for you?" I said to her.

"Nothing. I just didn't know any better," she answered.

"Really? Perhaps you didn't have the power to initiate sex, but you always had the power to refuse it—even if most of the time you didn't. And that kind of power isn't worth very much once you start initiating sex too—because then he can refuse you too."

Traditionally, this "Right of First Refusal" has been a woman's source of sexual power going back to her earliest sexual experiences. In almost all cases, she was the one who unilaterally decided with whom and when she lost her virginity. And in most marriages, she has retained this control ever since: She rations sex. It is her prime unit of exchange. When she "gives in," she is entitled to her husband's gratitude, and perhaps even some favor. And when she refuses his sexual advances, she is "keeping him in line," letting him know who is the ultimate sexual boss. Brenda, in her way, had been as much in control as Louis. That night upset the power balance for *both* of them.

"Hold on!" I can hear some of you protesting. *"You are describing some ancient tribal arrangement here, not a modern marriage. The days are long gone when women traded sex for marriage and fur coats. This is a demeaning view of women."*

I agree: It is a demeaning view of women. And of men too. And I wish it were not so accurate. But the fact remains that in most marriages—modern and otherwise—it is still the man who actively initiates sex the majority of the time. And it is still the woman who maintains the right of refusal. Time and again women come to my office complaining that they do not enjoy sex only to discover that they are *unwilling* to enjoy sex because if they did, they would relinquish their sexual control over their mates: A woman who actively enjoys sex can no longer claim to be giving in.

In true sexual equality, both the man and the woman relinquish power. Each has the right to initiate sex. And each has the right to refuse it. But making the transition to this kind of genuine sexual equality is no easy task. It is easier for most of us to get onto the Sexual Seesaw.

The fact that both Louis and Brenda had come all the way to New York to seek help showed that half their sexual-power battle was already over. They both wanted their marriage—and their sex—to work. My task was to help them get started again. As usual the first assignment I gave was Touching Exercise #1 —one caresses and fondles the other for up to three quarters of an hour, genitals and breasts off limits, no orgasmic sex allowed afterward. Because getting them started *in any way* was most critical, I told Louis to be the *active* partner—the caresser—the first night; I was convinced that asking him to be passive right away would be too much of a threat to him. As it was, that first night was hardly a success.

"I didn't feel anything," Brenda told me at our session the next day. "I just felt like a lump lying there. After a while, it was actually boring. For both of us. I told him to quit after fifteen minutes."

Louis agreed.

For the moment I dropped the matter. I knew that their mutual accumulation of anger was preventing them both from getting into the experience and as long as they were holding on to their anger, they could not turn themselves on. At the end of the session, I took out two string bags filled with Ping-Pong balls and handed one to each of them.

"Tonight I want you to duel at ten paces throwing Ping-Pong balls at each other," I told them. "Only one rule, you have to be nude. Later, if the spirit moves you, you can try the touching exercise again."

I could tell the moment they came into my office the next day that things had gone better—much better.

"We cheated," Brenda blurted out, unable to hide her smile. "We made love."

By venting anger physically—but harmlessly—they had opened the door to making love for the first time in almost a year. But this alone had not begun to right the imbalance which had caused their problem in the first place. They had not yet crossed the bridge to the place where either one of them could initiate sex, so I asked them to try Touching Exercise #1 again, this time with Brenda as the active partner and Louis as the passive receiver of pleasure.

"Resist temptation," I warned him. "Don't try to touch her back at all. If it helps, close your eyes and pretend it's a geisha girl massaging you."

For men who feel threatened by the idea of being sexually passive—and that category seems to include most men—the fantasy of being pleasured by a geisha or a masseuse makes things much easier. In fact, most men frequently have the fantasy of being "taken care of" by a geisha; it is only in real life that they find this idea threatening. But Louis seemed willing to give it a try; it was Brenda who was resistant.

"I'm not sure I want to be his geisha," she said.

"You can be anything you want," I told her, "but Louis can pretend you are anything he wants too. It's the touching that is important, and the pleasure you both derive from it. Let your bodies make friends first. You can talk about who you are and how you feel later."

Their bodies did make friends that night. It is a source of continuous wonder to me—even after all these years as a sex therapist—that simply touching and being touched can solve so many of our problems. Once we allow ourselves to feel another touching us, it is difficult to stay angry at that person. Once we relax under our partner's caress, the question of who is "in control" or of who "initiated" seems irrelevant. All that seems relevant is that *it feels good*—both to touch and to be touched.

For the first time in his life, Louis allowed himself to be passive—to let Brenda initiate sex and to carry it through. And he very happily admitted that it felt wonderful. Progressing through each of the touching exercises until they were alternating bringing each other to orgasm, Brenda and Louis rediscovered the most basic of sexual truths: *It feels good.* And it is only we, ourselves, who get in the way of these good feelings.

Throughout these exercises, I had insisted that they always alternate initiating sex and at their last session I asked them to make a deal—with me as their witness—that once they were back home they would continue to alternate initiating sex.

"Not fair," Louis said with a smile. "She still owes me for the fifteen years when I did all the initiating."

The Middle-aged Man's Guide to Lazy Sex

Some things do change between the sexes, thank goodness. And one very noticeable change I have seen in recent years is women's willingness to openly admit that they want sex and that they want more of it. Unfortunately, this change has brought its share of problems too. I see an increasing number of married women who complain that their husbands have become sexually lazy, that the men do not have enough sexual energy to keep up with them.

One woman said to me, "I'd always thought it was a myth that a woman's sexual appetite keeps increasing while a man's peaks at twenty and starts going downhill from there. But now I'm willing to believe it."

"Don't," I cautioned her. "Only believing it can make it true."

The fact is that healthy women *and* men can have active and frequent sex well into old age. Perhaps most men take longer to reach orgasm in middle age than when they were younger—something both they and their wives appreciate; and perhaps it takes middle-aged men somewhat longer to become rearoused after orgasm—but the difference here is one of minutes or hours, not days or weeks. No, a man who hides behind middle age as the reason for his flagging sexual appetite is fooling both his wife and himself. It is not sexual energy he is lacking—it is something else.

Much of Part I of this book deals with the various things that "something else" could be. But here I want to note one rather overwhelming Sexual Seesaw which has found its way into many contemporary marriages: With married women suddenly saying that they want sex and that they want more of it, married men are suddenly saying, "Not tonight dear—I'm too tired."

The reason once again, I suspect, has to do with a man's sense of sexual power. The very same man who acts sexually lazy in the marriage bed can go through an entire day outside of his home feeling sexually aroused as he flirts in the office and

fantasizes on the train. He is "lazy" *because* his wife openly
wants sex; it deprives him of his role as sexual aggressor and
pursuer. And without this role to play, he does not feel very
sexual at all.

Historically, in most cultures the males have been the sexual
aggressors; the image of the caveman dragging his mate by the
hair to the marital cave lingers with us. Intercourse itself seems
to symbolize male dominance: *He* penetrates *her*. His is the
position of dominance. But in today's world, the notions of male
dominance and female submission seem less and less relevant.
And when a woman openly admits that she wants more sex with
her husband, it is often too much for him. He shrivels—literally
and figuratively. It is one thing not to be the aggressor anymore,
but it is another to be in bed with a "Voracious Woman."

Once again, men tend to see women in extremes: If she is not
sexually coy or reticent, then she must be voracious and insatiable. Either she is a "Prim Princess" or she is an amazon. Nothing
in between. Many men's fear of a "Voracious Lover" runs deep;
it calls up the terrors of childhood and an overwhelming
mother. A voracious, insatiable lover will eat him alive. It
reaches down to one of his most terrifying fantasies: Of being
swallowed up in his wife's vagina, like Jonah in the Whale.

But hold on! All these wives are saying is that they've discovered they really like sex. And that they want it more frequently
and want to initiate it some of the time too. Does that make
them insatiable?

"I guess I'm just having trouble getting used to it," one husband said of his wife's new sexual openness. "But all she has to
do is say something like 'Boy, I could go for some good-old
loving tonight' and the panic sets in. The only way I can calm
myself is by fantasizing that I'm seducing the young woman
who lives next door."

No wonder his fantasy is calming: In it he is the aggressor, the
seducer, the taker of the virgin. For a man like him, any marriage will require some sexual adjustment because his wife cannot become a virgin again and again every night of their married life. But he tends to see all of sex as a performance and any
sexual request as a "Command Performance," an overwhelming demand. We will talk more about the kind of problems he

runs up against and how he can begin to overcome them in Chapter 5. But for now, let us see how he and his wife have polarized one another. He sees her as a Voracious Lover and backs away from sex in a panic; she, in turn, sees him as a "Lazy Lover," a middle-aged man with "Waning Powers," and tries to goad him into sexual action. The more she goads, the more he panics. Seesaw.

There is one exercise I recommend for depolarizing a couple who have gotten onto this particular seesaw. I call it "The Middle-Aged Man's Guide to Lazy Sex":

For one month, the wife can ask for sex whenever she wants it —up to twice a day—and her husband must accept. *But he is allowed to satisfy her with as little effort as he wants to put out.* He can lie back, stare at the ceiling, and masturbate her with one hand if that is all he feels like. And she, in turn, should not complain that he is lazy: She is being satisfied.

This is, of course, a paradoxical exercise. For most couples, it is only a matter of weeks before the husband discovers that his wife is not really all that insatiable—it only seemed that way when he was begging off so much of the time. Furthermore, he may soon find that with the pressure of performance absent, he is ready and willing to do all kinds of things that he had been "too tired" for earlier.

This is an exercise I can heartily recommend to any couple who have even a hint of this kind of imbalance and consequent polarization; it can put them both on the way to calm and caring sexual equality. But for many of us, there are steps to be taken before we can attempt this exercise: We must be ready to accept sexual pleasure "selfishly"—something which is especially difficult for women; and we must be willing to be satisfied with sexual variations other than sexual intercourse, a problem for many married couples. Later we will explore ways of getting over both of these hurdles.

Make Anger, Not Love

When one partner refuses to make love, it is often because he or she is angry about something and does not want to "give in" to sex. Anger and fighting are a component of every marriage; how that anger influences sex can determine how well a marriage thrives.

"We can be in the middle of a rip-roaring fight," Janice G., a newly married young woman, told me, "and all of sudden Brian will say, 'This is getting us nowhere—let's hit the sack!' Just like that! He thinks sex will solve everything. But damn it, when I'm mad, I'm mad, and the last thing I feel like doing is spreading my legs."

"Does 'spreading your legs' make you feel like you've lost the fight?" I asked her.

"You bet it does," Janice answered.

"Then maybe we ought to figure out some ways you can have sex and still come out a winner," I said.

In general, I am partial to Janice's husband's point of view about anger and sex: Verbal fighting can take you so far and then it just seems to feed off of itself—it does get us nowhere. And sex has the possibility of cutting through anger, providing a release for it, and taking both partners to a new plane of feeling and understanding.

It is very difficult, of course, not to let anger get in the way of sex. Yet on the other hand, we too often let love get in the way of sex too. We think that we always have to feel tender toward one another to have sex and so when we are feeling angry, we don't "give in" to sex. The very term "making love" is loaded: Perhaps there are times when it is more appropriate to "make anger" than to "make love." The important thing is that you do it.

"Making anger" is not really so strange or perverse an idea. We all recognize those film scenes—*Gone with the Wind* has a classic one—where a man and a woman abruptly break off in the middle of a violent fight and suddenly grab one another in a passionate embrace. The emotional transition makes intuitive sense to us: *Anger* and *arousal* come from the same part of us. They are both expressions of excitement, stimulation. They are both products of a passionate interaction with one another.

At the most primitive level, *anger, fear,* and *sexual arousal* are the same. When a male dog is frightened, one of its first physical responses is to get an erection. Similarly, humans become sexually aroused at various times of excitement: A woman overcome with laughter may find later that she has lubricated in her panties; a man overcome by grief may have a lingering erection for hours. And it very well may be appropriate to have sex with our partners at any of these times—as a purely frivolous extension of a moment of laughter; as a passionate link to life at a moment of grief. *Sex does not have to be one thing, an expression of just one emotion.* To impose that limitation on ourselves guarantees us sexual boredom. The fact is, when one partner screams, "I'm too angry to have sex!" he or she is probably sexually aroused already. The question is, what have we got to lose by giving in to this feeling of arousal when we are angry at one another?

For too many people married sex simply does not allow for "making anger," just as it does not allow for frivolous, playful sex either. No, married sex must be "serious" sex—just like Mom and Dad used to have. "Making anger" seems too risky, too dangerous—*too passionate*—for married life. Thus, we limit our sexual opportunities to those moments when we share just one small part of the spectrum of emotions we feel: moments of tender love. And then we complain that we don't make love often enough.

For others, like Janice, the young woman I mentioned above, moving from anger to sex, from a fight into bed, feels like losing an argument. As I came to know her and her husband, Brian, I began to understand how she could feel that way. Brian had a dominant personality and a fiery one; he had grown up in a home where fighting was a daily way of life and he did not take his fights with his wife that seriously. But in the middle of a fight when he suddenly suggested that they "hit the sack," he was not merely trying to transcend their argument with sex, he was using sex as a control—to distract Janice, keep her "busy," and to ultimately reassert his dominance over her. And Janice felt this. For a while, whenever Brian had initiated sex in the middle of a fight, Janice had reluctantly given in. She put it this way:

"I'd say to myself, 'Okay, I'll have sex, but I won't respond. I won't give him that satisfaction.' But after a while I felt like a double loser. Not only was Brian having his way, but he was having all the pleasure and I wasn't having any."

To Janice, each and every fight with Brian was a cataclysmic event: She saw each one as a threat to their relationship, a sign that there was something fundamentally wrong with their marriage. She had grown up in a family where fights were rare and she did not yet understand that fighting can be a part of the rhythm of marriage, a way to ventilate feelings and provide "vacations" of healthy distance between them. Rather than being a threat to her relationship with Brian, fights could very well be the "glue" which held it together. But as long as she saw sex as "losing an argument," there was no way she could view their fights as a possible bond.

"When I'm angry at Brian, he just seems like a rotten person to me," she said. "And how can I make love to a rotten person? I mean, what does that make me?"

"It seems to me that you are still yourself whatever you think Brian is at the time," I told her. "But as long as sex at these times makes you feel overpowered by him—like a child—I can certainly understand why you won't give in to your sexual feelings and allow yourself to respond to him. But instead of simply having you avoid sex or not respond at these times, let's try to find ways you can feel in control of sex."

I suggested to Janice that the next time Brian initiated sex at a time when she was angry at him, she should willingly go along with him, *but that she should take charge:*

When he enters you, hold him tightly inside you. Feel that you are *clamping him*, not that he is *penetrating you.*

Next, I suggested that she work out her anger physically in sex:

Get on top of him, in the "superior" position, and feel how *you are pinning him down.* Take charge of the movement. Let the thrusts of your pelvis express your anger.

Janice, quite naturally, was reluctant to try these exercises for some time. She was not used to feeling so assertive—sexually or otherwise—and she was afraid of how Brian might respond. But finally, in the midst of a fight, Brian once again suggested that they "hit the sack."

"I was furious," Janice told me, barely able to suppress her smile, "and I said, 'Okay, let's get at it!' He didn't know what was going on. And once we got into bed, he didn't know what hit him! I did everything we talked about and it was marvelous —for me at least. It was the best sex I've had since we got married. He was more stunned than anything, I think. But afterwards he was like a little puppy and somehow we both felt so close to each other that a little while later we made love. First we made anger, then we made love."

It is a good combination. In time, Janice and Brian were fighting less but enjoying it more. In sex where each partner is in control, there are no losers. And one simple truth remains: It is hard to remain angry when you are giving one another pleasure.

"Let's Make a Deal"

For both partners to want sex at the same time or with the same frequency is a major problem in married life. Yet whenever I tell a couple that "sex is negotiable," they react in horror.

"You make it sound so cold and businesslike," they say. "We want romance and you're talking about transactions," they protest.

"I'm talking about both of you getting what you want," I answer, "from romance to orgasms. And waiting for that just to 'happen' can take the rest of your lives. You don't have to negotiate *while* you are having sex—that does not sound like much fun at all. But negotiations certainly are a good way to get sex started."

For most couples, once they get into it, negotiating their sex lives can actually be fun.

"It's kind of like playing a sexy game of 'Let's Make a Deal,'" one woman told me.

For couples with unequal desires of frequency—that is, roughly ninety percent of married couples—I suggest a very simple kind of deal-making which goes something like this: "I'll make love more frequently—say, three times a week—if you promise to spend more time touching me first—say, a whole hour."

"Okay, but with the lights on."

"It's a deal!"

These "Wish Exchanges" can extend to all parts of your relationship, from the way you want the "mood" for sex to be set to a particular sexual variation which you have always fantasized about, but were too timid or afraid to ask for. Once one wish is out, the others seem to follow more easily:

"I've always wanted to be met at the door by a smiling woman with a drink in her hand."

"And I've always wanted to be carried into the bedroom and made love to for hours."

"I've always wanted you to kiss my chest and belly."

"And I've always wanted you to talk to me while we make love."

If we truly listen to one another's wishes and make an honest deal we can live with—for one night or one week—we are well on our way to a fulfilling balance in our sex lives. And there is nothing cold and heartless about that.

3
Family—the Biggest Turnoff of Them All

There is a story which one of my psychology professors liked to tell which went like this:

A middle-aged couple sat down in his office for their first session and he asked them what had made them decide to come for sex therapy. The couple looked nervously at one another for a moment and then the man said, "You tell him, Mother."

The story is a joke, of course, but it underscores the single greatest cause of sexual unhappiness in marriage: We identify our spouses with our parents—wife with mother, husband with father—and then we find that we do not feel very much like making love to them.

It is older than the story of Oedipus and as old as the incest taboo, but nowhere do we feel the inhibitions of this infamous neurotic confusion more than in the marriage bed. Enough has been written elsewhere about the Oedipus complex and the Electra complex and the various stages of childhood sexual development—I will not presume to cast new light on classical theory here. But there is a very simple and fundamental observation about Family Love and Sexual Love which is too often overlooked—perhaps because it is so fundamental: We learn, as a matter of normal development, to turn off sexually to our loved ones—to Mom, Dad, Sister, and Brother—in the family we are born into. And then when we marry and create a family of our own, the taboo is rekindled: *We once again turn off to our loved one*—our husband or wife. *Family* Love precludes *Sexual*

Love. *The one person we have chosen to love and make love to for the rest of our life is the one person we have often "learned" to turn off to.*

It is remarkable how many people tell me that their sex lives were just fine—*until they got married!* Before, they had marvelous, sexually uninhibited affairs, often including an affair with the person they eventually wed. But the moment they took their marriage vows they turned off. To cite an extreme example: I have seen countless women who were orgasmic right up until their wedding night and then they suddenly found they were incapable of orgasm. Another extreme example: I have seen many men who functioned perfectly sexually until the birth of their first child and then, with their wife now a mother, they suddenly had bouts of impotency. These are the extremes, but my guess is that at times all of us have experienced the sexually deadening effect of Family Love. *Making hot, uninhibited love to the one we love turns out to be the last taboo.*

How did we end up with this awful sexual confusion?

"You tell him, Mother."

Mom-and-Dad Sex

Moms and Dads do not make love—at least that is what many of us want to believe as children. It is a belief born of necessity: It keeps us from feeling left out, from feeling that we are less than Number One in the competition for Mom's or Dad's affection. And our belief, in most cases, is reinforced by the secretiveness of our parents' sex lives: We never *saw* them make love; some of us never *heard* them; in fact, most of us cannot even remember one time when Mom was late getting downstairs to make our breakfast because she was lingering in bed with Dad, and if she did stay up there with Dad, we block out the memory. (Much has been written about the damage done children who had to sleep in the same bedrooms as their parents and thus witness their lovemaking; but little has been mentioned anywhere about the damage done children because they were brought up *totally unaware* of their parents' lovemaking, as if "responsible" mothers and fathers were perfectly chaste.) Even as adults most of us have difficulty imagining our parents making love: The very idea makes us giddy and more than a little bit apprehensive.

When we finally learned the "facts of life," it dawned on us that Mom and Dad must have made love at least a few times—but solely for the purpose of creating us children. Sex, we learned, is for procreation—not for fun. Thus Mom-and-Dad Sex is a very serious business: serious, purposeful, responsible—everything but joyful.

And so when we marry and become "Mom" and "Dad" ourselves, we lock into a pattern: We start having Mom-and-Dad Sex, as distinct from all that frivolous, free, purely recreational sex we experienced when we were single. The spirits of Mom and Dad hover over our marriage beds like punishing angels, whispering in our ears, "Hey, not too much fun there, this is serious business. You're a Mom and Dad now too."

"It's amazing," one young woman told me, "but the very night I got married I suddenly got kind of prim about sex. I mean when I walked into the bedroom, I covered myself with a robe—I'd never done that in all the years I was single. My husband thought it was a joke, that I was playing the 'virgin bride,' but I just felt this was different. Sex had to be *meaningful* now that we were married."

"And no fun?" I asked her.

"Well, not *just* for fun," she said. "Not anymore."

For Mom-and-Dad Sex to be "meaningful," it must always be an expression of love—preferably of lifelong, abiding love—every time we climb into bed with one another. And what an incredible burden that is! It eliminates sex stimulated by a whole array of other emotions and sensations: *Playful sex* and *angry sex, quick, "mindless" sex* and *"naughty" sex*. It eliminates, in fact, just about every occasion for having sex there is. After all, who can feel "lifelong, abiding love" that regularly—especially at eleven o'clock at night?

It is little wonder that those of us who become locked into Mom-and-Dad Sex look back on our single sex lives with yearning—a yearning which can all too easily lead us to extramarital affairs instead of to ways of breaking out of our Mom-and-Dad roles. *Because extramarital sex, like premarital sex, does not invoke the ghosts of Mom and Dad.* No, by its very definition sex outside marriage is illicit and so it allows us to have free, "naughty," recreational sex—sex just for fun.

But there is no reason why any of us has to become Mom or Dad the moment we marry, no reason why we have to limit ourselves to "serious" married sex the moment we start our own families. We are still sexual beings with a whole range of sexual feelings after we slip the wedding rings on our fingers; we are still capable of playful sex and angry sex and even "naughty" sex in our marriage beds. If we are willing to examine how we get trapped into our Mom and Dad roles, we can take the first step to breaking out of them—and start having sexual fun again.

Just Like the Girl Who Married Dear Old Dad

The trap is set by the very sound reasons why we opt for marriage in the first place. For the majority of us today, sex in itself is no longer the prime reason for marriage: After all, sex is available to most of us without wedding bands and pledges of eternal loyalty. No, it is these pledges themselves we yearn for; after the insecurities and emptiness of transient relationships, we want the comforts, security, and continuity of a committed relationship. And we want a family.

As one man I know put it, "It's a scary world out there. I've got a stressful job, I'm in competition all day, and nothing at all seems permanent—not even the earth itself. I just got tired of having uncertainty in my social life too. I finally got married because I wanted one fixed point in my life—a safe and caring place to go to at night. I wanted to go home."

It sounds reasonable enough, doesn't it? And yet this same man was in my office because after less than two years of marriage he had drifted into sexual apathy.

"I look at my wife," he said, "and I say to myself, 'I truly love that woman. She is everything I ever wanted—a perfect life-

mate.' The question is, why aren't I turned on by her anymore?"

"Maybe a 'safe and caring place' is not a very sexy place to
you," I said. "Maybe it is too much like *home.*"

At home, we want to be stroked and comforted; we want to
come in from the "scary world" and be told that "everything's
going to be all right." And a loyal and loving wife or husband
will—and should—be able to do that for us. But if that is the
main component we focus on in marriage—"Comforting Love"
—we are, like Oedipus, tempting the Fates. We are asking our
wives basically to be our mothers and our husbands to be our
fathers and then we find we are not turned on to them anymore.

Turning ourselves off to our real mothers and fathers is a
fundamental lesson in survival that we learn as children. We are
not allowed to have Mommy and Daddy as our partners, so we
take the first step in controlling our sexuality: We numb ourselves to our sexual feelings for them. It is part and parcel of our
sexual development and in one way or another this lesson lingers with us throughout our adult lives. At its best, it allows us to
control our sexual urges when they are inappropriate; at its
worst, it keeps us from expressing our sexual urges when they
are most appropriate—with our husbands and wives.

For some, the worst of this lesson comes into play with the
very choice we make of a spouse. Consciously or unconsciously,
we may place "sexually attractive" partners into one category
and "marriageable partners" into another.

One woman told me, "I knew the moment I met Rob that he
was the man I wanted to marry—but I was never really turned
on by him."

She might very well have said, "I knew I wanted to marry
Rob *because* I was never turned on by him." She was choosing a
marriageable partner on the basis of what she unconsciously
thought a proper husband should be: Someone she was not
turned on to. A husband is family and you are not supposed to
be sexually attracted to a member of your family. Yet this
woman had come to see me because she found her married sex
life so dull.

For many men, the distinction between "marriageable" and

"sexually attractive" parallels their fundamental separation of women into either "madonnas" or "whores." A "madonna" is just like the girl who married dear old Dad: She is good and pure—she is "above" sex. And "whores" are purely sexual: That is *all* they are good for. Obviously, it is the "madonnas" these men marry; at least that is who they *think* they are marrying. But many of them soon discover that their "madonnas" are sexual too—they actively want sex—and then these men are doubly turned off: They do not want to make love to a "whore" in their marriage bed, especially in the room next to the children's.

Some of us consciously seek a mate who reminds us of Mom or Dad, someone who is similar in everything from looks to occupation. The song "I Want a Girl Just Like the Girl That Married Dear Old Dad" may sound alarmingly innocent to us now, but its sentiment is still very much in practice. And there is nothing necessarily wrong with that either. But time and again I see women in my office who married "a guy just like Dad" and now they cannot let go sexually with him. For many of us it is difficult to get out from behind these early learned inhibitions and to make open, free love with "a guy just like Dad."

There are those of us who go to the other extreme too: We choose mates precisely because *they do not remind us of Mom or Dad.* The so-called "attraction of opposites" is rooted in our desire to find someone who does not trigger our "family" inhibitions. In Sweden, I knew many men and women who were only sexually attracted to and married foreigners—the darker the better: An Italian husband is not likely to remind a Swedish woman of her blond Papa.

But whom we choose for a mate is only half the story. What we—and marriage itself—makes them into is the more telling half.

The Hot-Water Bottle
That Killed a Marriage

In the sixties film *Diary of a Mad Housewife,* the husband (played by Richard Benjamin) catches a cold which ruins his marriage. Between sneezes, he yells from the bedroom for aspirin, moans for cough syrup, screams for more Kleenex—for a fresh hot-water bottle! And his wife (played by Carrie Snodgrass) is in the hallway pulling out her hair. She has had it. She is tired of taking care of him, tired of his pathetic dependency. She does not want to be his mother; she already has children: *She wants a man!* The next day she starts having an extramarital affair.

All too often, women who were once taken by their husband's "charming boyishness" come to me complaining that they cannot stand living with an overgrown child. Certainly there are times—and perhaps a cold may be one of them—when we have to "mother" our husbands and "father" our wives. It comes with the territory of marriage. But too many of us slip into the roles of mothering and fathering our mates virtually all the time. It becomes the only way we see one another. And it is not a very sexy role for either of us.

"The moment Larry walks in the door, he pulls this hangdog look on me," Martha G., a young housewife, told me. "And that look says, 'I've had a terrible day—take care of me.' I don't really mind bringing him a drink or rubbing his shoulders, but after about five days in a row of that, I feel like screaming, 'Shape up! I've been a mother all day. I don't want a wimp—I want a man! I want romance!' Just once I'd like him to walk in the door, take me in his arms, and give me a passionate kiss. Instead, I get a peck on the cheek and that famous look of his."

Martha went on to say that their sex life was infrequent and lackluster.

"At eleven o'clock on the button, he says, 'Let's go to bed,' but I can't make the switch that fast. Presto chango from his mother to his lover. Sex feels like one more duty I have to perform—like doing his shirts and getting the car lubed. He hardly looks like Prince Charming to me."

Interestingly enough, her husband, Larry, saw their roles as the same, but for a very different reason:

"Martha runs the house like a tight ship and she is very definitely the captain. Coming home is like stepping into enemy territory. She says, 'Wipe your feet' and 'Hang up your coat' and 'Dinner will be ready in exactly fifteen minutes.' It's my mother all over again. Here I've been running a business all day and when I come home I'm treated like I'm seven years old again. And then she complains that I'm not passionate enough. Who can be a passionate lover when you're seven years old?"

Without realizing it, Martha and Larry had collaborated with one another in sustaining their roles as "mother" and "child." But there was a third party to this collaboration: Marriage itself. The very structure of marriage prepares us to see our wives as "mothers" and our husbands as "fathers"; the only other wife and husband we ever saw at close quarters were our own mothers and fathers so the identification is a natural one. When we create our own families and our wives become the mothers of our children and our husbands their fathers, that identification is reinforced. Furthermore, the custom of calling our mother-in-law "Mother" reduces the husband-wife relationship to a nonsexual family relationship: If we both call her "Mother," then we must be brother and sister. And brothers and sisters, just like children and parents, must not turn on to one another.

In traditional homes (more later on homes where both partners work) the spheres of duty and responsibility are prescribed to press the wife into the role of "Mother," the husband into the role of "Father," and both into the role of the other's "Child."

"As soon as we got married and moved into our own apartment, I felt like I was living with my mother again," one man said to me. "She makes me dinner, she knows where my socks are—she even picks out my clothes for me. Not only that, but she tells me to change my underwear, not to bite my nails, and to take out the garbage. Good Lord, the only time I ever felt like an adult was those five years as a bachelor between my parents' house and this one."

Within four years of marriage this man's sex life had become all but nonexistent—he could only get aroused by fantasizing about another woman. Then he began having extramarital affairs.

"I had to," he insisted to me. "Out of self-respect. To feel like a grown-up again. To feel like a man."

He went on to tell me an anecdote that would be comical if it were not so sad as well:

"She knew I was having affairs, but she never said anything—only pouted every time I went out the door. Then one night just as I was about to go out, she said, 'You're seeing another woman, aren't you?' And I said, 'Yes. I am.' Well, for a second I thought she was going to cry, but suddenly she started wagging her head and she said, 'Well, you can't go out looking like that, you know. Not with that shirt on!' "

Mothering was the only role this woman had ever learned and it was not entirely her fault. She, her husband, and marriage itself had conspired to polarize them into these roles. The only way he felt he could get out of his role was by getting out of his house; the only way she felt she could hold on to him was by mothering him into submission. Both positions were dooming their sex lives—and their marriage—to failure.

In traditional homes, the husband all too frequently slips into the role of "Father" to his wife too. He is the one who usually makes and manages the money just as Father used to; he is the one who is most connected to the outside world; and most importantly, he is the one who has to be pleased and who dishes out words of approval and disapproval. In one of Dory Previn's most penetrating songs, "I Danced and Danced," she recounts how, as a child, she used to dance for her father to see him smile and now, as a woman, she is still "dancing" for her husband.

"Somehow I always manage to fall into the trap of being Bill's fawning, overeager little girl," Marilyn L., a 30-year-old Washington wife said to me. "I'm always showing him something I've done and then waiting to see if he's going to be critical or not. Usually he's critical, of course."

Marilyn had come to see me because her orgasms had become less and less frequent.

"When he gets on top of me and starts to make love, I sometimes feel like I can't breathe," she told me. "I feel smothered by him and all I can think about is that I want it to be over so I can breathe again."

Living with a critical "father" is frequently smothering; it certainly is not conducive to free, responsive sex. "Life with Father" is not very sexy at all.

And yet again, when I spoke with Marilyn's husband, Bill, a government attorney, I saw that he was not alone to blame for his role of "Father" to Marilyn's "little girl": "She's always depressed," he told me. "She's always saying something like 'I can't get anything done' or 'I'm getting fat,' and I'm supposed to hug her and say, 'No, you look great, honey.' But after a while I just turn off and turn away. I mean if someone tells you often enough that she's losing her looks, you start to believe her. I get tired of being Big Daddy who has to cheer her up and handle her with care. I can't tell you how much I long for a confident, sexual woman who thinks she's beautiful—a woman who can take the rough and tumble of some real sexy sex instead of this delicate stuff Marilyn wants."

Again, we see two people who have locked themselves into a parent-child relationship and with this relationship has come a failing sex life. A wife who always acts like a man's mother will often find him acting like an inhibited, undemonstrative, and certainly unromantic child in bed; and a man who routinely treats his wife like his mother will frequently find that she is losing sexual interest in him. Likewise, a man who primarily acts like his wife's father is apt to find her a reluctant, nervous lover after a while; just as a wife who repeatedly "asks" her husband to assume the role of "father" in too many ways may soon find him drifting into sexual apathy.

Roles die hard. In modern marriages where both partners have careers and both share in the business of running the home and raising the children, one would think that we had a better chance of avoiding the roles of each other's "mother" and "father." With the husband cooking supper and the wife carrying a briefcase, the simple role identifications would seem harder to make. But, alas, once the dishes are washed and the children are in bed, we too often slip back into the old archetypes—especially in the bedroom. Suddenly, the "equal partner" husband is in desperate need of some maternal comfort:

"God, what an awful day I've had," he says, and presents his back to his wife for a much-needed massage. Never mind that she has had an awful day too and needs "mothering" herself.

Or the wife, a high-powered executive by day, stands in front of the bedroom mirror and says, "I'm losing my looks. Look at me—I look like a worn-out shrew," and suddenly the confident woman of the world whom her husband has been looking forward to making love to seems to need a reassuring Big Daddy hug more than some hot and heavy sex.

And, frequently, despite protestations that they have a modern "equal partner" marriage, the husband is a male chauvinist in disguise: He cooks supper, but he also insists that he run their finances, even though his wife has an MBA and a job on Wall Street.

"In the final analysis, he's really no different from my father," one angry wife told me. "He's just a chauvinist pig in sheep's clothing. And that's not the kind of man I want to share my bed with."

To be sure, we are talking in extremes here. Inevitably we play the roles of "Mother" and "Father" to one another some of the time; as I say, it comes with the territory of marriage. And inevitably, the particular "Mother" and "Father" roles we witness in childhood families—say, a domineering mother and a passive father, or a frustrated mother and an insensitive father —will influence the roles we adopt in our own marriages. But the *degrees* to which we play these roles are critical—particularly when it comes to making the transition to each other as lovers.

How to "UnMommy" Your Wife and "UnDaddy" Your Husband

The process of "UnMommying" our wives and "UnDaddying" our husbands begins in our minds, where the confusion started: First, it would be foolish to try to convince ourselves that we are going to totally exclude our "Mommying" and "Daddying" roles from our relationship. These roles, after all, are part of the reason we got married in the first place: for the comfort and security it affords us. But we must see that being a "maternal comfort" to our husband is only *one* of the roles we can play—*one of many*. And it does not have to exclude other roles—the roles of friend, co-adventurer, and *lover*. Mature men and women can learn to make the transition from "Mommy" or "Daddy" to "Lover" without having to feel confused or guilty.

Fundamental to making this transition is learning how to merge affection and sex. For too many of us, affection signals Family Love to the exclusion of Sexual Love. There is no better case in point than *kissing*.

What ever did happen to kissing in married sex?

An occasional Mom-and-Dad peck, yes—but what about those lovely, lingering, open-mouthed kisses of our premarital days? Why should they now make us feel so uncomfortable and nervous?

We seem to desensitize and "sanitize" hugging and kissing once we are married. We make them all comfort and no sensuousness like the chaste kisses we saw Mom give Dad at the door. There was a time in most of our lives when we could hug and kiss for hours on the front porch or in the back of the car and tingle with sexual excitement—and we are still those same people with those same sexual feelings, yet we have turned them off. "Affection" is one thing, we seem to have decided, and "sex" is another. Sex has to do exclusively with breasts, clitorises, and penises—and maybe a kiss when the sex is over—and affection has to do with fully clothed, quick hugs and kisses like the ones we give our children.

Kissing can make us more sexually nervous than intercourse itself. Face-to-face, lips-to-lips, and eyes-to-eyes, we seem to be in more intimate contact than when just our genitals are touching. We think of our "Selves" as living behind our eyes and when we kiss, our "Selves" make contact: There can be no fantasizing about another person, no "fogging" of our identities. We are making direct and intimate contact with each other. As we will see in Chapter 6, kissing may make us feel "too close for comfort"; but it also brings into sharp focus our anxieties about having sexual contact with a member of our family—even though that family member is our spouse.

The problem seems to be both men's and women's. We were so used to turning ourselves off when we kissed and hugged our parents, and now when we kiss our children, that we continue to turn ourselves off when we kiss and hug our spouses. We fail to see affection and sex as a *continuum*. Yet holding our husbands in a comforting "everything's going to be all right" hug can very easily slide by degrees into a feeling of sensuous body contact. Instead of merely feeling the hug as our "wifely/maternal" duty—something we do *for* our husbands—we can feel the pleasure it gives *us:* The gentle pressure of their heads or chests against our breasts, the sensual feeling of their lips and breath on our necks. It is a question of allowing ourselves to switch the focus, of catching ourselves before we automatically turn off. Try to remember that this hug, this kiss is *exactly the same physical act* which once made us delirious with sexual excitement; the *act* has not changed, only what we allow ourselves to feel has.

For many men, accepting affection can be very nervous-making. They were less used to it as boys than girls were and they are less comfortable with it now than most women are. The last place where boys receive physical comforting from their mothers is usually the neck and back and these remain the least threatening parts of the body for affection to begin in adulthood. It is a question of *sliding:* from shoulders and back to chest and belly, from affection to sensuality to sex. They are all part and parcel of the same thing: making each other—and ourselves—feel good.

When Martha and Larry G. (the couple who had locked themselves into the roles of comforting, boss-of-the-home "Mother" and needy, demanding "Child") came to see me, their sex life was at a virtual standstill.

"All he wants is a pat on the head and someone to listen to what a rotten day he's had," Martha told me. "It's no wonder I'm turned off to him. When I hug him, I feel like I'm hugging another one of the kids. I want some passion in my life; is that too much to ask?"

"Not at all," I answered. "And it is not too much to give

either. But you have to begin with where you are now and move into passion from there. Larry is not suddenly going to appear at the door in a cape and sweep you into his arms any more than you are suddenly going to start wearing black stockings and a low-cut blouse to meet him at the door—although changing out of a house dress and apron might be one good place to start: They even make you *look* like a mother."

But instead of screaming, *"I'm not your mother!"*—something Martha never could have gotten herself to do in any event—I suggested that she give Larry all the mothering he wants *before* he asks for it, before he presents her with his familiar hangdog look.

"Don't make him drag it out of you," I told Martha. "Don't make him go into his 'beaten child' routine. Pat his head, listen to him for fifteen minutes, and then say, 'Okay, now it's *my* turn. Let me tell you about my day.' "

By taking this tack, Martha could begin to free *both* of them from their roles without denying that Larry did indeed need *some* comforting—but not an entire evening of it. She could say to him, in effect, "Okay, *both* of us need some 'mothering' some of the time, but let's not let it get out of hand. And let's not keep it *so one-sided."*

Larry, for his part, felt there was no way he could be more of a "man" if the minute he walked into the house he felt he was trespassing on "enemy territory" where his wife, like a mother, was in full control. He wanted life at home to be a little less orderly, a little looser, and a lot less controlled.

"You'll never break out of your role by *asking permission* to," I told Larry. "If you feel like a child when you ask where your socks are, then don't ask. Grow up and find them yourself. Stop repeating the way you acted with your mother. Take charge of your socks yourself. You cannot have it both ways. Ultimately, no one is making you feel unsexy but yourself."

Further, I tried to get Larry to accept the idea that he could take and give affection in a sensual frame of mind, that "Comforting Love" could lead very naturally into wonderful sex.

The first assignment I gave Martha and Larry was an Un-Mommying Exercise designed to re-create Comforting Love in a *sexual context*. Rather than trying to avoid their "Mother/

Child" roles, I wanted them to break through them, leaving their residual guilt behind them. I told Martha:

Give him all the "mothering" he wants, but *you* choose the setting—and make it a sexual setting. Lead him by the hand to the bathroom, draw a warm bath, and undress him. Bring him a drink if he wants one. (This time "Mother" does not bring him a glass of milk; she brings him a martini!) Scrub his back and neck and shoulders while he unburdens himself. But *think sexually* while you are doing all of this. Change into an attractive robe or swimsuit while you "mother" him—his real mother never looked like *that!* Allow yourself to take pleasure in soaking and stroking his body. Move to his chest, his belly—gradually—giving you both time to relax with the sensuality of what is happening.

As always with these exercises, orgasmic sex does not have to follow—not even genital contact. But sensuality will be established. Martha was able to merge her "Mothering" role with her "Lover" role without denying either of them. And Larry, once he was able to adjust to this turnabout, was able to accept Martha's affection without feeling desensitized by it. In fact, after a few weeks, he was feeling very sensitized by this exercise.

"The fifth time I led him into the bathroom," Martha told me happily, "he pulled me into the tub with him."

Another UnMommying Exercise which I've found to be effective confronts our locked-in roles even more directly and takes them to the extreme:

Let your husband stretch out on the couch with his head on your lap in the classic "Madonna and Child" posture. Stroke his hair and face, rocking him gently as you would a child. Perhaps even murmur reassuring words to him, hum to him. Let him talk, if he wants. Most important is that he feel relaxed and secure.
But both of you allow yourselves to see and feel the inherent sensuality in this position. His head is near your breasts; when you rock his head, feel the pressure of it against your breasts.

Do not automatically turn yourself off. Do not say to yourself, "We are not in the right position—in the right moods or roles —for sexual feeling." Get beyond the fixed idea that this is a weak, unsexy position for a man to be in or a smothering, unsexy position for a woman to be in.

Begin, slowly, to reach into his shirt and softly touch his neck and chest with your fingertips. You are conveying to him that you find him attractive in this position too, just as, by responding, he shows that he is enjoying receiving pleasure. Now you may both be ready to press his head very deliberately to your breasts—perhaps to unbutton your blouse and pull his face to them.

Your husband should know that he can pull his head away if he wants—if it feels too demanding or threatening at first. He can close his eyes, back away, and come back as often as he likes.

The Madonna and Child Exercise confronts a basic sexual anxiety literally head-on. For a man to put his face close to his wife's breast in the classic "Mommy and Child" position allows him to gradually overcome his fear of being "mothered to death," of being smothered in his "mother's" bosom. He is able, finally, to transform his wife's breasts into sexual objects which he is allowed to enjoy. In the end, UnMommying our wives does not have to make them less "Mommyish"—it simply makes them *sexual* too.

In a similar way, we can UnDaddy our husbands. Again, we do not deny the role, but we merge it with our other roles. We let "Father" and "Lover" mingle together so we are not locked into any one way of seeing one another.

For some men, the role of Big Daddy *is* very sexual to begin with. It affords them total control—and hence is no sexual threat to them. They can be the sexual teacher and critic; they can be the ones who "need to be pleased." But the "Big Daddy/ Naive Little Girl" combination rarely endures in a marriage. In time, the husband gets tired of the "little girl" passivity and wants a responsive, confident woman in bed with him. And "little girls"—especially after they are married—have a tendency to "grow up" and have active sexual needs of their own.

Marilyn and Bill L. (the couple who had locked into roles of "Doting/Insecure Little Girl" and "Critical/Handle-With-Care Big Daddy") had both drifted into sexual apathy by the time they reached my office. Marilyn felt that she "could not breathe" when they made love: "All I could ever think about is 'Am I doing it right? Is this the way he wants me to move? Does he think I look sexy?' I am so busy trying to please that the last thing in the world I think about is how it feels to me."

Bill, on the other hand, felt paralyzed by Marilyn's childlike insecurity. He said he longed for the "rough and tumble" of sex with a "real" woman: "I always have this feeling that I have to be so careful when we make love. And I have to keep whispering words of encouragement—'That's great, honey; you're doing wonderfully'—stuff like that. And, of course, I have to keep reassuring her that I love her and that she looks beautiful. Sometimes I just want to get at it!"

Again, the UnDaddying Exercises I suggested to Marilyn and Bill were designed to exaggerate their roles, not avoid them. By recreating ways that Bill could give Marilyn Big Daddy support and encouragement *in a sexual context*, I could help them merge Comforting Love and Sexual Love:

Cradle her in your arms and rock her like a little child, all the while reassuring her that you love her. And when she seems relaxed and content, carry her into the bedroom and put her on the bed.

Massage her gently, telling her this is just for her—she doesn't have to do anything in response. Gradually turn your encouraging remarks about the way she looks into sexual advances. Go from "You *do* look beautiful, honey" to "I would love to run my hand up your legs." Your partner, in turn, should allow herself to drift on her sexual feelings, to feel herself the object of your sexual desire.

By not having to respond, Marilyn was able to recontact own sexual feelings for herself and at the same time to feel attractiveness to Bill: Big Daddy could be Lover too. Bill, or other hand, could refocus on Marilyn as a sexual, desirable desiring body.

I told them that whenever they found themselves in
Big Daddy/Little Girl situation to look for its sexual pote
see how they could make the transition from Family Lc
Sexual Love. Much to Bill's surprise and pleasure, Marilyn
to this idea with a great deal of inventiveness.

"She had been begging me to teach her how to drive m
sports car which has a floor shift," Bill told me, "so one evening
we went out to a country road over in Virginia and she got in
the driver's seat. I really didn't have sex on my mind at the time,
but after a while I noticed that she was hiking her skirt farther
and farther up her thighs. Then I saw she had a coy little smirk
on her face. She saw I was looking at her legs and she slipped
her hand from the gear shift into my lap. 'Is this the way you do
it?' she said. Wow, what a lesson we had!"

In both UnMommying and UnDaddying, the trick is to allow
ourselves to be children again—but now we are children who
can go "all the way." Once we feel secure in our ability to move
from one role to another, we can play any sexual games we want
to; and many of the best games are children's games. I know one
couple who broke through the "Father/Child" barrier by playing out the "Forbidden Game" of an older man teaching a
younger woman about sex. "What's that?" she would say in all
wide-eyed wonder when he undid his pants. "I'll show you," her
husband would answer. Other couples I know can relax sexually
by talking baby talk in bed. True adults are comfortable with
regressive sex; they are not afraid of being playful. By being
children in bed, we can break through the taboos which inhibited us as children. And we can have better sex than Mom and
Dad ever did.

4
The "Real Thing"

Recently, Amy and Bill P., an attractive couple in their early
fifties, came to see me about what they called the "disastrous
turn" their sex life had taken. They were terribly distraught.
For almost thirty years, they said, they had enjoyed a fulfilling
sex life, but now Amy, as the result of a recurring vaginal infec-
tion, found it too painful to tolerate the insertion of her husband's penis.

"The frustration is just killing us," Bill said. "It's almost a year
now since we've had any sex together and it's taking a terrible
toll on our whole relationship."

I looked at the two of them. They were both intelligent, well-
educated people with interesting jobs and a sophisticated circle
of friends. Over the years they had traveled together to every
corner of the globe, getting to know firsthand a fascinating
variety of cultures. Even their knowledge about sex was impressive—they had read everything from the *Kama Sutra* to Freud's
collected works. Yet this couple had fallen victim to the most
simplistic sexual myth ever perpetrated on Man—and Woman.
The myth that sexual intercourse is the one and only "Real
Thing," the only "proper and mature" mode of sex for married
couples.

"Tell me," I said, suppressing a smile. "How many more children were you two planning to have?"

For a moment, both of them stared at me as if I were stark
raving mad. But then they simultaneously broke into great

gales of laughter. It was laughter of recognition. And it was laughter of relief. Because my little joke was the first step in getting them to give themselves permission to go home and enjoy modes of sex other than sexual intercourse.

Of course, Amy and Bill (the parents of four grown children) were not planning on having any more babies at their age. Yet sexual intercourse—the *reproductive mode* of having sex—was all they had permitted themselves in thirty years, even long after the reproductive phase of their life together had passed. If Amy and Bill were not able to do the "Real Thing," well, then they were not going to do anything at all.

Amy and Bill's story illustrates just one of the ways that the myth of the "Real Thing" invades our sex lives, limits us, and ultimately causes sexual boredom to set in. Even at the other end of the spectrum, with couples who occasionally allow themselves *nonreproductive-mode* sex—say, oral sex or mutual masturbation—the myth persists, making one or both partners feel guilty, demeaned, or abnormal. The myth seems to take its toll on everyone, but no one suffers from it more than married couples.

Sex and the Single Groove

There is a concept in modern psychology and anthropology known as "remnant behavior." A good example is the way a dog or cat will walk around in a circle a few times before settling down on a rug: It is behavior left over from its ancestral days in the wild when circling in the high grass created a little space in which to lie down. Sexual intercourse as the *one and only way* many of us allow ourselves to enjoy orgasmic sex in marriage is another example: It is a leftover habit from the days of yore (not so long ago, really) when sex and reproduction were indivisibly connected in marriage, from the days when life expectancy was short, infant mortality high, and sex was totally directed toward procreation. But unlike the cat circling on the rug, ours is not a quaint and harmless habit—it can reduce our sex lives to a single groove.

Before I go on, I guess I had better respond to those people yelling in the back row, *"Are you really trying to tell us that sexual intercourse is passé?"*

Not at all. Nor am I saying that it is the worst sex there is. Or necessarily the best. I only want to make the point that sexual intercourse is just *one of the many ways* a couple can experience sexual pleasure together, just one of the ways a couple can reach orgasm. And that if we reduce ourselves to one way—any one way—we may be dooming ourselves to the gloom of sexual boredom.

It is not hard to figure out how we get stuck with single-groove sex in marriage. People of all monogamous cultures know instinctively that the primary purpose of a lifelong commitment to one mate is to create children and to be secure in our knowledge that the children are ours alone, that there is no question for *either* partner about who their children's father is. It is the basis of the Virginity Taboo (that a woman must remain a virgin until she marries) and, though that taboo is not nearly as rigorously adhered to as it once was, its remnants linger on.

The Virginity Taboo assured a man that he was the father of the first child his wife bore, just as later, the Infidelity Taboo discouraged a man from begetting (and having to support) children with any other mate. The rule, simply, was that you were allowed to have sexual intercourse only with your mate. But here, somewhere in the recesses of our minds, we made a quizzical jump: We went from the idea that *we are allowed to have sexual intercourse Only with our lifelong mate* to the idea that *the Only kind of sex we are allowed to have with our lifelong mate is sexual intercourse.* The two ideas, "sexual intercourse" and "lifelong mate," are wedded in our minds like "love" and "marriage." You can't have one without the other. And you can *only* have one—*one kind of sex*—with the other.

For many couples, the end result is sexual monotony. Stuck with just reproductive-mode sex, these couples sink into frustration and boredom. Most have active fantasies of enjoying a variety of sexual activities, and soon resentments can set in, then dreams of infidelity—if they cannot enjoy sexual variety with one mate, then they want a variety of sexual partners. But either one or both of them simply cannot overcome The "Real

Thing" Myth; they cannot let go of the idea that married sex should be "mature," "serious," and "responsible." And that it shouldn't be too much fun.

Can Mom, the Church, and the Alabama Penal Code All Be Wrong?

Fighting The "Real Thing" Myth is like fighting city hall. There is an impressive array of authorities who are bent on keeping the myth alive and well and on keeping our sex lives dull. It begins with the biggest authorities of them all, our parents (what doesn't begin with parents?) and includes our childhood friends, the Church, several state laws, and, as if that were not enough, many psychoanalysts as well.

Even the most enlightened, liberal parents who sit their kids down for some frank sex talk manage to convey the message that there is only one *real* way that sex is done: The penis goes into the vagina, makes its little deposit of seeds, and that is how babies begin. That is the whole idea of sex, we are patiently informed as children—*to make babies.* Sex *is* reproduction.

"Oh sure," some parents may add shyly, "it *does* feel good, but that is only Nature's way of ensuring that the species keeps reproducing."

With this bit of information—our first authoritative sexual knowledge—many of us grew up not only believing that there is only one *real* way grown-ups have sex together, but also believing that Mom and Dad probably only did it five or six times in their lives—once for brother, once for sister, once for us, and maybe a couple of times when it didn't work. So begins the Joylessness of Sex Education.

The guilty secret that parents never seem to reveal to children is that sex is one of the great pleasures of life—*even when it has nothing at all to do with making babies.* It is certainly hard to imagine any parent explaining to a child that there are many different ways people can enjoy sex—not just sexual intercourse —and that each of these can be delightful in its own right. This simple, harmless piece of information might have set us on a course toward a varied and guilt-free sex life when we grew up. As it is, most of us reached sexual maturity believing way deep down that there is something wrong, dirty, or abnormal about sex which is totally unrelated to reproduction.

There is no better case in point than masturbation. For the great majority of us, masturbation was our first active sexual experience. But rare indeed is the child who did not begin (at some point) to feel guilty about this solitary pleasure. Even if there was no parent who told you that it was a "dirty and vile" practice, who warned you to "keep your hands *on top* of the blankets, darling," or who hammered on the locked bathroom door yelling, "What on earth are you doing in there all this time?"; even if you hadn't read in the *Boy Scout Handbook* that it was an "unmanly" habit or hadn't been solemnly informed by some young neighborhood sage that it made warts grow on your hands, stunted your growth, or turned you into a "pansy"— even without any of this guilt-inducing propaganda about masturbation—most of us would have succumbed fairly soon to the idea that there is something grossly unnatural about the practice. After all, what could be further from reproduction than having sex alone? *That* is the real sin; *that* is the first and foremost reason for all our guilt—we are doing it simply for our own pleasure, not for sex's *real* purpose—to make babies.

In adolescence, when we begin our first forays into the world of partnered sex, The "Real Thing" Myth is reaffirmed in a paradoxical way. Instead of sexual intercourse being the only form of sex *allowed*, it becomes the only form of sex *denied*. At best, it becomes a special favor bestowed by a young woman on a deserving young man. And thus for many—especially teenage boys—intercourse takes on the status of the Ultimate Achievement. To an adolescent, "doing *it*" or "going all the way" means only one thing. And anything other than "going all the way," even if it includes petting to orgasm, mutual masturbation, or what was once called "dry humping," is construed as incomplete sex, pale substitutes falling far short of the Ultimate Achievement.

The irony here is double-edged. Because all these "pale substitutes" for the "Real Thing" in which adolescents indulge are precisely what so many adult couples I know yearn to be doing *now.* They would give anything to recapture the slow titillation of petting for hours in the backseat of a car, the visual wonder and exploding orgasms of mutual masturbation, the reckless romance of "dry humping." Yet these adult couples are stuck with their version of The "Real Thing" Myth: Married Sex = Sexual Intercourse—*and nothing else.* Sexual intercourse goes from being the only thing you *can't* do in adolescence to the only thing you *can* do in committed, adult sex.

But let us stay with these adolescents for a moment. Because before I go on to demonstrate how a prohibitive society limits our sexual options, I have to admit that there are some ways in which all these restrictions actually expand our sexual horizons. An adolescent kept from "going all the way" is forced to experience all these lovely substitutes—even if he or she does feel cheated. Slow and sensual petting is a lesson a teenager will be glad he learned when the routines of "Real Thing" Sex start to get dull later in life. Growing up in the permissive society of Sweden, I saw too many teenagers go from 0 to 100 sexually. Their very *first* sexual experience was intercourse. No dallying with petting or any other "substitutions"; these were considered "kinky" and "unhealthy." They went straight to the "Real Thing," which Swedish society saw as "healthy" and "proper." As a result, Swedes—despite the popular American myth to the contrary—are generally quite limited in their sexual repertoire. No sexual smorgasbord for them. In a study I made of Swedish men who had had sexual experiences with American women, these men said that their American lovers were much more fun than those at home.

"American girls are harder to get into bed," one told me, "but once they're there, it seems there's a lot more to do."

Unfortunately, the effects of a prohibitive society are not limited to our adolescent sex lives. Organized religion goes a long way in perpetuating The "Real Thing" Myth throughout our adult lives. From the Old Testament warning against spilling one's seed on the ground to the prohibitions of most modern Christian religions, the message is loud and clear: The Divine Purpose of sex is reproduction and sex not directed to this end is sinful. In some ways, the Catholic Church appears more liberal on this issue than several other religions: It permits some sexual variety as long as it all ultimately leads to sexual intercourse. Still, the Vatican's prohibition against contraception says it all.

I truly do not want to involve myself in a theological argument about Divine Purpose here: I am hardly qualified for such an argument and we sex therapists have enough trouble as it is avoiding the label of "Devil's Helpers" when it comes to sex and religion. My only point is a question which you have to answer for yourself:

Do you honestly believe that you and your partner should experience sex only when it leads—or might lead—to conception? Do you only indulge in sex for this purpose and never use any form of contraception?

For most of us the answer, of course, is no. Yet, as we will see, this answer alone is no guarantee that we are free of the inhibitions and boredom-causing limitations of The "Real Thing" Myth.

There is a secular argument that is roughly the same as the Divine Purpose argument and it goes like this: Sexual intercourse is the "natural" way to have sex. That is what the vagina is for, why it is built that way, it is where the penis belongs, and putting it anywhere else is "unnatural."

Again, the answer is "Yes, that is where the penis goes if you are making babies." But there are a great many people who enjoy the most "natural" pleasures without just putting it "where it belongs."

Consider two other pillars of society who try to convince us that there is only *one legitimate way* to experience sex: lawmakers and psychoanalysts, a truly unlikely pair. There are a number of American states which still carry laws on their books which make oral and anal sex between consenting adults—even married couples—illegal acts. These laws are rarely implemented, but the power of this prohibition put into law gives weight to our suspicion that there is something "not quite right" about sexual practices other than "normal" intercourse.

Sadly, early psychoanalytic theory joined in the campaign to limit our sex lives to sexual intercourse alone. According to such theory, our sexual practices and preferences are often seen only in the context of stages of "normal" development, relegating a predilection for oral sex to persons "fixated" at the oral stage of development and suggesting that a man's interest in experimenting with anal sex with his wife is a sure sign of latent homosexuality. The underlying credo is that fully developed people should be interested in "mature" sex only—the "Real Thing." Such theories, I think, are too facile. They do not take into account almost everyone's desire to experiment and our need to keep our lifelong relationships alive and exciting through the options of sexual variety.

Making Babies Versus Making Whoopee

Easily a third of the couples I see have sexual problems directly related to the issue of reproduction. Either they are afraid of making a new baby or they are afraid they will not be able to make one.

"I'm so terrified of getting pregnant," one mother of three told me, "that I can never really let myself go. I hardly ever have orgasms anymore. Halfway through sex I'm already planning my escape route to the bathroom so I can douche right away."

"I don't think you're trying to escape *to* contraception," I told her. "I think you're trying to escape *from* it—from admitting to yourself that you can enjoy sex which has nothing to do with reproduction."

One father admitted to me that when he thinks his wife is ovulating he cannot keep his erection. And countless couples have complained to me when we discuss methods of contraception that "it just doesn't seem worth all the hassle."

Admittedly, there are some couples who have not had the opportunity to learn how easy and effective modern contraception used properly can be; and once given this information, they can happily go home and get on with their sex lives. But there are many more couples who have *actively avoided* learning about contraception, who *irrationally distrust* it to work, or who join the chorus of "it just doesn't seem worth the hassle."

In virtually all of these cases the couples were really expressing their guilt about indulging in nonreproductive sex. They had unconsciously avoided learning about contraception because going to Planned Parenthood, to a sex-education course, or to the wife's gynecologist would have made them *too conscious* of the fact that they were actively seeking a sex life of pure pleasure and not one of making babies.

In a similar vein, women who tell me that they do not trust any contraception to work effectively are usually telling me that they do not *trust themselves* to use contraception properly. There are an astounding number of bright, well-educated women who manage to get pregnant—and have an abortion—year after year. They say that contraception "just doesn't seem to work" for them, but when pressed they admit that they "forget" to take their Pill or insert their diaphragm, that in the heat of passion they "don't want to interrupt the natural flow" of sex. One of these women finally confided to me that the only time she had satisfying orgasms was when she knew there was a chance of getting pregnant. For all of these women—from the mother who *could not* have orgasms because she was afraid of getting pregnant to the young wife who *could only* have orgasms if she thought she might get pregnant—The "Real Thing" Myth is actively at work preventing them from enjoying recreational sex for its own sake. They simply cannot allow themselves to separate Making Babies from Making Whoopee.

These are the extremes, yet for most of us the business of contraception is a source of some inhibition in our sex lives. We say that putting in a diaphragm is too messy, that the smell of the vaginal gel is a real turnoff, that the whole procedure of interrupting foreplay, getting out of bed, scurrying to the bathroom, and putting the "dumb thing" in is enough to make both of you "lose the mood" and call it quits.

"By the time I get back to the bedroom," one woman told me, "my husband has lost his erection and is usually reading the paper or watching TV. Let's face it—it *does* interrupt the flow of things. It's just so mechanical and so contrived. It's about the most unromantic thing in the world and it happens right in the middle of sex."

The true "lack of romance" about contraception, I suspect, is that putting in a diaphragm or rolling on a condom is a very clear and indisputable reminder that what we are about to do is to deliberately indulge in *nonreproductive sex*. The popularity of the Pill and of the coil (before many stopped using them because of possible side effects) was due to the fact that we did not have to think about contraception when we were in the mood for sex—in other words, we did not have to be reminded that what we were about to do had nothing to do with reproduction.

I can hear you protesting already: *"Nonsense! Putting in a diaphragm is messy! And it does break the mood! It brings the whole thing to a standstill!"*

But it does not have to, honestly. The hassle of contraception is mostly of our own making—it is yet another way that guilt gets us to turn ourselves off. The fact is there are a number of easy ways to get around this hassle:

Perhaps the easiest way is to routinely insert your diaphragm every day at the same time, say in the early evening just before or after dinner. Most vaginal gels remain active spermicides for five or six hours so the whole evening is safe for sex. Never mind that you haven't had one thought about sex all day. And as for the messiness, is it really any messier than brushing your teeth or shaving your legs? Make it a routine and you can forget about it and enjoy uninterrupted sex whenever the mood strikes.

I hesitate to recommend this method to all couples. Those for whom infrequency of sex has become a matter of tension and anxiety may come to resent putting in a diaphragm night after night and rarely using it. The diaphragm becomes a depressing reminder of how little is happening between you and your partner. And for a man who is vulnerable to seeing signs of "sexual demand" everywhere, knowing that your diaphragm is in and you are "ready to go" may be enough in itself to make him wither with performance anxiety. (See Chapter 7.) But there is a more general and telling reason why I usually only recommend this method as a *temporary* way to cut through the hassle of contraception: It does not bring us any closer to overcoming our anxiety about enjoying nonreproductive sex. Like the Pill and the coil, it just helps us avoid that whole issue.

I have found that there is no better way for couples to become fully conscious of the emotional distinction between Making Babies and Making Whoopee than to *make contraception a sensual part of sex play:*

Instead of keeping your diaphragm tucked away in some secret corner of the bathroom, let it live right next to your bed—in the drawer of your bed table or dresser. And when it looks like you are going to want to use it—when sex play has already begun—just reach over, take it out, and *insert it in full view* of your partner. Believe me, it will become anything but a turnoff for most men; in fact, watching you slowly insert it will probably be the most tantalizing of turn-ons for both of you.

The next step is even more erotic: Both of you put the diaphragm in together. Take your time. Slip it in and out as many times as you like. Remember: This is a *part* of foreplay, not a commercial interruption. After a while, many husbands will want to do it themselves—there is nothing more marvelously regressive than "playing doctor." And for those women who have spent a lifetime desperately trying to keep themselves from being turned on by gynecological examinations, it is a chance to indulge a secret fantasy. (Of course, for couples who use condoms as contraception, the same procedure goes: Put it on in front of her or better yet, let her roll it on for you.)

By sharing the responsibility for contraception in this way, many women feel less resentment about having the responsibility for taking precautions. But even more important, by making contraception a sensual part of sexual play, we focus on the true reason we are using it: so we can have pleasure, pure and simple. And in this way, we take a first step toward desensitizing ourselves to our guilt and anxieties about the pleasures of nonreproductive sex. By letting contraception be open and natural—not to mention sexy—we can very simply acknowledge to ourselves that tonight, at least, we just want to make whoopee.

There is one other method I like to recommend for making peace with contraception. It is more of a little family joke than an exercise but it was passed on to me by a charming middle-aged couple who swore it eased sexual tension for them every time:

> Whenever one of them wants to initiate sex with the other, she or he smiles and says, "Do you want to make babies tonight?"
> To which the other replies, "Hell, no!"
> "Terrific!" comes the response. "Let's have fun!"
> And off they go to bed.

Sadly, there are an increasing number of couples with sexual anxieties because they are having difficulty conceiving a child. For them, sex and reproduction all too quickly become one and the same thing. Every time they have sexual intercourse, it is fraught with apprehensiveness—"Will we conceive at last tonight? Is it the right time? Is my sperm count high enough? Am I ovulating?" Little wonder that sexual problems often set in— the joyous act has become a purely anxious one. There is also little wonder that couples battling infertility reduce their sexual variety to sexual intercourse. Having sex any other way seems a missed chance and wasted sperm. Many of these couples stop having sexual contact altogether under such duress and often the entire relationship begins to tear. Like any couple, these couples make the distinction between sex for procreation and sex for recreation. And my first step is to encourage them to have all kinds of sex *except* sexual intercourse for a while to regain the sense of sex for pure pleasure. Because sex without pleasure can curtail sex for reproduction before it even begins.

Again, these are the extremes: Couples with sexual problems specifically related to the issue of reproduction. But these problems derive from the same myths and confusions which affect us all. Making Babies Versus Making Whoopee is only half the story of The "Real Thing" Myth: It describes the anxieties we feel about sexual intercourse which does not lead to conception. The other half of the story is the way we limit ourselves to *reproductive-mode* sex—to only sexual intercourse—even when the business of reproduction is the furthest thing from our minds and lives.

"But Not with My Wife . . ."

In fact, a great number of modern married couples have had exciting sexual experiences which were anything but the "Real Thing"; they just haven't had these experiences *with each other* —at least not since they were married. They have tried all those "wild and crazy" things *before* marriage or possibly even during marriage *with other partners*. It seems it is okay to experiment in bed—or in the backseat of a car—with anybody but your lifelong, committed mate.

"Sure, I've tried just about every variation in my day," one husband told me with a mixture of pride and confusion, "but, hell, not with my wife. That exotic stuff just wouldn't feel right with her."

"Why not?" I said. "Are you afraid she might like it too much?"

For this man, as for so many people, exotic, experimental, purely recreational sex equaled nonmarital sex. In his mind, he could not do it *just for fun* with his own wife. After all, she is a mother—the mother of his children. And besides that, she is, well, she is *a lady*.

Here, Freud's classic Madonna/Whore complex again rears its ugly head: There are women to be used for sexual enjoyment and experimentation—women you could not possibly marry; and there are respectable, marriageable women—women with whom you could not possibly have frivolous, experimental sex. Whole cultures have built their sexual customs around this division; over the centuries Spanish men of wealth had their wives —with whom they had children—and they had their mistresses —with whom they had fun. To only a somewhat lesser degree this complex persists in our society. Perhaps few American men maintain mistresses, but too many of them still deny themselves purely recreational sex with the mother of their children: It "just doesn't feel right."

The Madonna/Whore complex is not exclusively a man's problem. There are a great number of women perfectly capable of enjoying sexual variations—perhaps even experienced in them—but who "just wouldn't feel right" having such adventures with their husbands, the father of their children. Several years ago, a Luis Bunuel film entitled *Belle de Jour* captured the sexual imaginations of many women I know. In the film Catherine Deneuve portrayed a woman in a very respectable marriage who spent her days as a call girl indulging in all kinds of exotic sexual games with her customers. Women told me that *Belle de Jour's* life matched their deepest fantasies; in other words, they saw themselves as either a whore who experimented with sex or a wife who didn't.

I have spoken to countless women who have active fantasies about oral sex and mutual masturbation but who have never once experienced these sexual variations with their husbands. As well, I have seen many women who keep these fantasies just below the surface of their minds only to have them come out when they talk with me or with a supportive group of other women. Several of these women told me that they would actually prefer these variations to sexual intercourse.

"I'd just as well skip intercourse," one of these women said to me. "I mean the boring part of intercourse with my husband is that I'm supposed to have an orgasm and he's working like crazy on me to have one. Yet it would, I'm sure, be nicer for me if we just petted and played with each other. Maybe had oral sex. The funny thing is I bet I'd have an orgasm easily if he just stuck to that."

"Probably the best way to start," I told her, "is by simply telling him that. You may be surprised: He just might be relieved to hear it." The truth is, surveys show that many women have orgasms more easily and more satisfactorily in oral sex and masturbation (mutual or solo) than in intercourse. Direct stimulation of the clitoris is more easily accomplished and a man's tongue and lips are gentler stimulators than his erect penis. Many women find these alternatives a welcome relief from all the anxieties associated with contraception.

Still, a great many women are inhibited about indulging in such sexual variations with their husbands. And many more are inhibited about simply *initiating* these variations—simply asking their husbands for them.

When I spoke alone with the wife of the man who said he "just wouldn't feel right" having "exotic" sex with her, she admitted to me that for years she had yearned to have oral sex with her husband.

"I can get turned on just fantasizing about it," she told me. "But all we ever really do is the same old routine—a short warm-up and then he comes inside me. It's like when it comes to sex we both go onto automatic pilot."

What a shame. Here were two healthy people both longing for some sexual variety in their lives and they were limiting themselves to the same unimaginative script that had brought them to the depths of sexual boredom.

Often, only one partner resists experimentation. It is not unusual for one partner to want to try a sexual variation—say, oral sex—but the other does not and this can be the cause of tremendous tension in a marriage.

"I'm tired of trying to badger her into just trying oral sex," one husband told me. "She always ends up making me feel like a pervert or something. She says all that stuff is for swingers and young people."

I turned to his wife. "Do you really think you are too old to try oral sex?"

"I guess I do," she admitted. "It doesn't seem to me like something mature people should have to do."

"Raising children takes maturity," I said, "but having sexual pleasure should be plain fun. When it comes to that, we're all the same age."

Still, I was as sympathetic to this woman's resistance as I was to her husband's desires. It is not easy to reach a mature age and suddenly try sexual experiments. The inhibitions surrounding oral sex in particular are difficult to overcome and I will devote a special section to them in Part II. But to begin, I wanted this woman to loosen up her thinking about "mature" sex—to see The "Real Thing" Myth for what it is.

"Hold on!" I can hear some of you objecting. *"What if both my husband and I are perfectly happy just doing the 'Real Thing'? Are you saying that we should try these variations anyhow?"*

Not necessarily. I don't think people should force themselves to do something sexually that they don't really want to do. But ask yourself honestly: "Have I ever had a sexual fantasy that included oral sex or mutual masturbation?" And if you have, don't you think you deserve to indulge these fantasies with each other—at least once?

Rare, indeed, is the person who has not had at least a flickering of one of these fantasies. But not so rare are those of us who "just don't feel right" about indulging them with our mates.

Going All the Way—but Another Route

Recently, I came across a passage in a book in which a young man who has just had his first sexual experience with a young woman is lying in bed musing about what happened:

"I wonder if I had been born in the wild if I would have known where to put *it*. I might have tried her arm pit first, or maybe her belly button. It's such an out-of-the-way spot really, hidden underneath everything. Maybe that was the first test of Natural Selection: those who put it in the arm pit didn't survive."

Whether or not we are born with the specific drive to "put it in the right place," we are certainly all born with the capacity to take sexual pleasure in any number of sexual variations which are not the "Real Thing." And given the opportunity and encouragement, many couples I have seen have happily and very naturally added these variations to their sex lives. For them it began with taking Touching Exercise #1 to its next logical step:

Touching Exercise #2

Again, take turns touching one another, but this time include breasts and genitals after you have touched/been touched everywhere else for at least forty-five minutes.

Take your time. Do not dive for the genitals. Treat them as you treat every other part of the body. And when your genitals are being touched, place your hand over your partner's hand. Guide him or her. Show what feels good—where you are sensitive, how fast, how slow.

Allow yourself to be brought to orgasm either manually or orally—any way *except* sexual intercourse. Avoid the temptation to "finish off" with the "Real Thing."

For many couples, this exercise proves extremely liberating. It may be the first time they have experienced orgasm outside of sexual intercourse and for once they are focused completely on their own pleasure.

"I felt so daring," one woman told me after she had tried the exercise with her husband. "It was as if we were breaking all the rules. And for some reason, it made us both feel young—like adolescents heavy-petting in the car. It's crazy, but I had a better orgasm than I usually have in intercourse."

It was not crazy at all. For once, she was just having fun.

5
Tonight's Performance Has Been Canceled

John G. came into my office with a scowl on his face. He was a tall, dapperly dressed advertising executive in his mid-thirties and he was furious. For five years he had had what he had assumed was a marvelous sex life with his wife, Ruth. But after making love one night a few months before, Ruth had blurted out that she hadn't really had an orgasm. She had just faked it. In fact, she admitted, she had faked it at least half the time since they had been married. John and Ruth had not made love since that night.

"It's like she's been lying to me all this time," John fumed. "I feel cheated."

"Do you consider yourself a good lover?" I asked him.

John smiled for the first time. "Yes," he said. "I think I'm pretty good at it."

"Maybe that's the problem," I said. "Maybe you're so busy trying to be a 'good lover' that there's no fun left in it for either of you."

After seeing John and Ruth, separately and together, a few more times, my suspicion was confirmed. John was a "Star Lover." He "performed" at sex the same way he performed at everything else in his life: with expertise, aggressiveness, and a need to impress his audience. For years Ruth had admired John's take-charge personality and without quite realizing why she was doing it, she had "applauded" her husband's performances with faked orgasms. But finally, in frustration and anger, she had canceled both their performances by blurting out her admission.

"I didn't consciously mean to hurt John," she told me, "but I guess I knew it would. I must have been angry at him because he had taken all the fun out of our sex. It's just that there didn't seem to be any *feeling* left in it for either of us. It's as though we were both playing these roles: John was Mr. Wonderful Lover and I was Mrs. Grateful Wife. But the funny thing is, there was nobody left to simply enjoy our performances."

Ruth's unusually perceptive insight ultimately saved her relationship with her husband. Yes, a great deal of hurt came first. During therapy, John finally had to confront his need to control and Ruth had to see that she had willingly given up on responsibility for her own sexuality. But after spending some time learning about themselves and each other, and after taking the time to relearn how to enjoy sex *from the inside out* instead of performing it *from the outside in,* they rediscovered simple sexual pleasure for its *own* sake.

But even if Ruth had not been the first to cancel their performance-oriented sex, John might very well have reached the same point of frustration on his own. Star Lovers, proficient and "expert" lovers, often eventually succumb to sexual apathy—especially in a committed relationship. They are usually the first to lament that the thrill is gone.

"Maybe I'm Doing It Wrong"

Randy Newman's hilarious song "Maybe I'm Doing It Wrong" satirizes the way many of us think about making love. We think there are people out there—the "experts" and the "phenomenal lovers"—who are "doing it right." They know all the right moves; their timing is impeccable (the men can last forever and the women have blockbuster orgasms, one after another); they are well practiced in a variety of exotic "tricks"; they can maintain a perfect balance between wild abandon and exacting control, and all the while they look as graceful and lovely as Nureyev and Fonteyn doing a pas de deux. Meanwhile most of the rest of us are "doing it wrong"—or at least we are not doing it quite as well as we should be.

Somewhere along the line we have acquired the idea that learning how to make love is in the same category as learning how to play tennis or speak French. It takes diligent study and lots and lots of practice. Earnest pupils pore over *The Joy of Sex*, illustrated "marriage manuals," and the *Penthouse* "Forum" searching for clues and tips on how to achieve sexual mastery. One man told me that he and his wife occasionally rented X-rated videotapes to see if they could pick up some "new techniques."

"You mean you look at them like educational films?" I asked him.

"Well, sort of," he said.

"Sounds pretty boring to me," I said. It did indeed. It sounded like watching *Casablanca* to learn how to mix drinks.

Even my mentors, Masters and Johnson, have inadvertently helped perpetuate the idea that making love is basically a series of techniques to be learned under a tutor and then practiced until you got them right. To be sure, Masters and Johnson's therapy is geared to help couples reestablish contact with their sexual feelings, but in the popular mind, Masters is the champion of mastery, the preeminent guru of sexual technique. He can teach us how to be Star Lovers.

I have this funny, old-fashioned idea that there is not all that much that most of us have to learn about the technique of making love. It is all pretty much the same as learning how to get to the airport in a new city—a couple of trips and you know basically how to get there. All the rest comes rather naturally. Now this may sound like a bizarre admission coming from a person who has spent the past fifteen years as a sex therapist. But my task with the great majority of the people I see is *not* helping them learn how to "do it right"; rather we spend most of our time trying to *unlearn* the myths and propaganda which have prevented us from simply feeling sexual pleasure. And at the top of the list of these self-destructive myths is the one that proclaims that making love is an "act" which requires expert mastery to be "performed" with finesse. Disarmed by this myth, we fault ourselves or our partners (or both) for not living up to expectations.

We have just come through one of the biggest sexual myth-making periods of all time: the so-called Sexual Revolution. Ironically the Sexual Revolution's mandate of "sexual freedom for all" soon became a compulsion of "sexual pressure on all." Not only were we told that sex was out there to be enjoyed whenever and with whomever we wanted, but we were told that if we did not take advantage of all this sexual availability we were "uptight," or worse, sexually backward. In this way, the Sexual Revolution produced millions of what I call "Phantom Lovers," men and women who felt compelled by social pressure to get out there and perform sexually even if they did not feel emotionally ready for it. Instead of coming to terms with their own fairly common sexual inhibitions, they raced pell-mell into the sexual foray, girding themselves with sexual techniques. Devoting themselves to sexual mastery became a substitute for learning how to relax with sexual pleasure. They became sexual "experts"; all that was missing was sexual feeling. Now, in the eighties, I am seeing the veterans of the Sexual Revolution and their biggest complaint is that they do not feel anything anymore.

"I learned everything there was to know about sex during the Sexual Revolution," one woman told me. "The only thing I neglected to learn was how to enjoy myself. It's almost as if I were impersonating a lover all that time. If I had been a fly on the ceiling of my bedroom watching all that thrashing and moaning going on below I would have seen myself as a terrific lover. But meanwhile down on the bed, I was just going through the paces, doing all the right things but never really just letting go and having a good time."

Goaded by the fad of sexual freedom, this woman was forcing herself to perform intimate acts for which she was not emotionally ready. In another era, she might have delayed sex until she had a better grip on her anxieties about men and sex; but in the midst of the Sexual Revolution she leapt into bed and kept men at an emotional arm's length by embracing them in unfelt passion. She was doing sex, not feeling it.

What all these sexual performers have in common is that they experience sex from the *outside in:* They *begin* with technique, with the right moves, the right look, the perfect control, while sexual pleasure—if there is any—is the *end result* of all this technique. But sex that *begins* with our sexual feelings—that focuses on our own sensations rather than on our performance —finds its own techniques.

The Score: Conquests 100, Pleasure 0

There is a theory that Don Juan wandered through the world seducing a different woman every night because he was searching for the one woman with whom he could enjoy sex.

As one of my colleagues put it, "Don Juan would have done better if he had just stayed home one night and masturbated. That way he could have enjoyed himself for once: He was so involved with controlling his sexual partners that there was nothing left for himself. He was all control and no pleasure. The conquest itself was the only thrill."

Sexual conquest—what some young men call "scoring"—is the ultimate Sexual Performance. It turns sexuality upside down: It makes the achievement of sexual intercourse an *end in itself* rather than making intercourse the *means* for achieving sexual gratification. And as is the case with most goal-oriented activities, Conquest Sex is a way that many men (and women too) avoid confronting their anxieties about the *process* of sex. Scratch a Don Juan and you will probably find a man who is guilty about simply enjoying sex.

Don Juanism is machismo carried to its extreme. From time immemorial it has taken a "Real Man" to seduce the "Elusive Virgin." His performance, like all good performances, begins with the right look and clothes, moves on to the right gestures (eye contact is all important) and right words ("lines" they are called, like an actor reading his lines) and culminates in the perfectly choreographed moves of "Star" lovemaking. Why is it, then, with all this perfection, that so many of these Don Juans' conquests turn up in my office saying that they could never really "let go" in bed with these Star Lovers?

"He was the kind of lover I always fantasized about," one woman told me. "He knew how to press all the right buttons at just the right time. And I *was* turned on at the beginning. But then I was overcome by this awful empty feeling and I kind of went cold. In the end I never came and he sort of got mad and the whole evening ended on a sour note. I felt terrible. It was like I had wasted this perfectly golden opportunity."

"What do you think was missing?" I asked.

The young woman thought quietly for a long time. "A real person," she said finally.

Yes, a real person.

For the goal-oriented Don Juans themselves, it usually takes much longer to track down their own "missing person." In the mid-seventies, an increasing number of these "conquering heroes" came to my office feeling sexually defeated. Many of them complained that sometimes they did not even come at all. For them, "lasting long" and making their partners come first (preferably several times) is the supreme sexual achievement. And thus sex begins and ends with control—control of their partners and control of themselves. The awful irony is that perfect control—lasting forever—means not coming at all: A "Perfect Lover" has no personal sexual satisfaction whatsoever.

I'm afraid it is a sign of the times that recently I have seen quite a number of men who have taken to faking orgasms themselves—a bit of acting which was reserved for women until now.

"There just reaches a point where I'm tired and want it all to be over with," one of these men told me. "By faking it, I get out of it gracefully, without my partner feeling bad."

Echoes of the "Grateful Wife."

Other men complained that they were losing their sexual interests and drive, that frequently they lost their concentration (and sometimes their erections) in the middle of lovemaking.

"It's crazy," one of these men sighed. "Sex has always been the biggest thing in my life. I love it. And now it's run out on me."

"I don't think it's run out on you," I told him. "I think you ran out on it a long time ago. You haven't been involved enough with your own sexual feelings. You have never really realized and just taken in sexual pleasure for your own satisfaction. It's not sex that's missing. You've been missing from sex."

In the midst of the Sexual Revolution, something else was suddenly missing for many of these men: the thrill of conquest. Now there was all this sexual availability; women did not need to be conquered, they were willing partners leading the way to their bedrooms. And all at once these men who were schooled and practiced in the arts of seduction and lovemaking had the rug pulled out from under them. They did not know what to do. They felt lost and confused and many of them felt emasculated. The sexual goal was gone and there was nothing left to replace it. So they—or at least their bodies—gave up on sex altogether.

When someone preoccupied with sexual performance gets married, something very much like this can happen. He has made his conquest and now she lies in his bed a willing partner forever after. And suddenly the thrill is gone. How can he possibly make love to the same person for the rest of his life?

The Job of Sex

A young, attractive couple, Jane and Edgar K., entered my office, both looking disconsolate. They had been married for four months and had only made love twice in that time.

"Before we got married, we used to make love three and four times a week," Jane told me. "But starting with our wedding night, our sex life has been a disaster."

"I think you're making too big a deal out of it," Edgar cut in nervously. "It seems a little early to be making judgments about our married sex life."

It was, sadly, a story I was familiar with: Sex had changed radically with the making of a lifetime commitment. There can be a variety of causes for this abrupt turnabout in our sexual relationships at the moment that a commitment is made. But with Jane and Edgar, I had a very specific sense of what had gone wrong: Jane had been a virgin when Edgar first made love to her, but Edgar had had a great number of sexual experiences with many partners before he met her. I suspected that with his

"Innocent Bride" conquered for life, Edgar's sexual motivation was gone. If he could not see Jane as a sexual conquest, he saw her as a sexual demand. And Jane was no help: She was still waiting for her "experienced lover" to take the lead. Edgar was stuck with the Job of Sex.

This flip-flop is all too common a factor in many marriages. Sex is seen in extremes: Either one is the "conqueror" or one is being "conquered"; either one puts in a Star Performance or a Command Performance—there is nothing in between. But at both extremes, the performer sees sex as something to do *to* or *for* his partner, not simply for his own sensual gratification.

Such a man often does not put in his joyless performance alone: Too often his thankless role is supported by a partner with high expectations—and critical reviews. The idea that a good lover lasts forever is reinforced by wives who complain that their husbands come too soon, who may even cry out when he ejaculates, "You don't consider me at all! You only think about yourself!"

It is a performance she is demanding, so it is a performance she will get. It rarely occurs to her that she can have her orgasm in ways other than through intercourse, that her insistence on his "doing it right" can doom them both to anxiety-ridden Performance Sex.

At the end of one of our first sessions, I suggested to Edgar and Jane that they try the nongenital touching exercises with Edgar lying perfectly still while Jane touched and caressed him.

"You've been the seducer all these years," I said to Edgar. "Now it's your turn to find out how much fun it is to be seduced."

It was not easy for Edgar to suddenly become a passive "enjoyer" after years of being an active "performer"; nor was it easy for Jane to become active and responsible for initiating sex after years of playing the coy little girl. For many sessions Edgar in particular resisted this turnabout: He said it made him feel uncomfortable and guilty. He said that he did not feel like a "man." But in time, he came to enjoy the pleasures of just relaxing and taking in sexual sensations for the first time in his life. The performer faded and the enjoyer emerged.

If men are the main sexual performers before marriage, it is women who frequently play roles after marriage. But theirs is not a star role, it is a supporting role. Even in this age of equal sexual rights for women, the myth persists in the minds of many women that *after* marriage sex belongs to the man and it is a woman's role to perform it to his satisfaction. It becomes her duty, her contractual obligation, her *Job of Sex*. The moment the wedding ring is on her finger, she gives up sex as her own selfish pleasure and begins her lifetime performance as the "Dutiful Wife."

"No way!" I can hear many young women protesting. *"That may have been true for our mother's generation, but not for ours."*

I only wish they were right. True, by the time they reach my office, many women—younger and older—have reached the point where they are sick to death of the Job of Sex. They are ready to quit. They want sex for themselves again. But before they reach that point, a great many women have already slipped into the role of Dutiful Wife without ever realizing that it was happening. Even in some of the most liberated marriages, where both partners are working and share in household tasks and child care, when it comes to the bedroom the old roles are still there: *Sex is basically for the man.* Nine times out of ten it is the man who initiates sex and if his wife refuses *she* is at fault, made to feel guilty with tactics ranging from sulky moods to browbeating threats. And on those rare occasions when she initiates sex, it is not her husband's contractual obligation to fulfill her. No, chances are she is gently reproved for overstepping her boundaries, for putting pressure on, for not playing her appropriate passive role. The communication of this idea may be subtle—just a hurt or disapproving look, a sigh, a long silence —but the message is loud and clear: Be a good wife—do your job!

Similarly, the choices of how sex will be done become the man's prerogative; he decides when, where, how long, what mode, what position. He may not verbalize his preferences (in fact, he probably does not open his mouth), but he is clearly in charge of sex. He is the "director" and she is the dutiful and willing "performer." The talk around the dining-room table may be about feminism and sexual equality, but the practice in the bedroom is often not all that different from Mom and Dad's.

And as we have already seen, a wife's role comes directly from Mom. Mom "took care" of things; she satisfied everyone's needs. She cooked dinner and cleaned the closets and sex was just one more of her duties. One woman told me that she remembered her mother retiring early one evening each week, excusing herself by saying, "I have to go up and take care of your father now." *Take care!* She was just performing another of her household duties. And Heaven forbid she should enjoy it.

Traditionally, sex was the way that a woman kept her man, kept him from wandering from home and kept him from getting depressed or angry. Performing sexually was the way she managed their relationship and managed her anxiety about their relationship. But all the while she was simply *doing* sex—putting in a performance—neglecting to have sex for her own satisfaction as well.

Implicit in this wifely role—be it an old-fashioned Mom or a modern-but-accommodating woman—is that sex is "giving in." It is a passive obligation, not an active pleasure. Certainly most women who "give in" every time their husbands initiate sex manage to enjoy themselves once they get started. But often they harbor a resentment, a resentment which can grow. Why is it always on his terms? When he wants it? What about all those missed opportunities when I wanted it?

Unless it is part of a mutually understood "please seduce me" scene (See Chapter 13, Only When It's Good), many women never truly enjoy sex when it is just "giving in." The very idea has a negative connotation. As a woman in one of my groups described it, "How can I have any fun when I know I'm just doing it to keep him from getting into a bad mood?"

One couple complained that they were never in the mood for sex at the same time because she only felt turned on *the day after* they made love.

"She's just obstinate," her husband told me with a smile, trying to make it sound like a little joke his wife played on him.

But it was no joke. As we discovered after a few sessions, this was a woman who could never completely take pleasure in sex when she was just "giving in." But as soon as she had her "duty" out of the way, she felt free to enjoy herself . . . the next day. It was the way she rewarded herself for doing the Job of Sex.

Paradoxically, many modern wives have more complex sexual roles to play than their mothers ever did. These young women do not dutifully traipse upstairs to "take care of Father" —a modern husband would not be happy if his wife just lay there passively. No, the modern wife must put in a "responsive" performance. She has to act as if she is enjoying it—whether or not she really is. Yet she cannot be *too responsive* or her performance will be regarded as "demanding," and some particularly competitive men become angry if their wives' "ecstatic" performances exceed their own. The perfect wife has to strike a delicate balance between "wild abandon" and Grateful Wife. And the high point of her performance must be her orgasm— again, whether or not she has one. She cannot risk her husband's disappointment or anger for failing to give him the ultimate sexual response.

Faking an orgasm is a good way not to have a real one. Just as putting in any other kind of sexual performance is a good way not to feel truly sexual. The Don Juans and Dutiful Wives are actually not so different from one another: Ultimately they both disassociate their inner feelings from the sexual "act." But the Dutiful Wife may very well have more than just a myth to contend with—she may have the ongoing pressure of a Hard Worker husband.

The Hard Worker in Bed

Some women who have been faking orgasms keep it a secret from their husbands while, through therapy and exercises, they learn to have real orgasms. In the end, when these women no longer need to fake it, the husbands frequently do not know the difference.

I allow my patients this exception to honest, nonperformance-oriented sex because there are some men who simply could not tolerate this news. It would break them and it would break their marriages.

In recent years, since the so-called "rediscovery" of the female orgasm, many performance-oriented men have become fixated on it. They have to give their partner "The Big O"—and they have to give it through sexual intercourse—or they consider themselves sexual failures. A "Perfect Lover" makes his partner come each and every time. It is both his burden and his reward. Little wonder that his partner often ends up faking it.

This preoccupation with a wife's orgasm is Don Juanism come home. It is the way performance mastery invades our marital bedrooms and often makes both husband and wife quite miserable. I have spoken to men who even became unfaithful because their wives did not have orgasms; they needed to prove their skills as lovers. And I have spoken to some men who lost interest in sex—or worse, became impotent—because their wives did not have orgasms. To these husbands, the fact that their wives are not having orgasms is proof positive that they are "doing it wrong." And every time they make love it is a reminder of what they consider to be their own sexual inadequacy.

One couple, Anna and Brian G., had arrived at this point by the time I first saw them.

"I just feel so guilty every time," Brian said despondently. "Like I'm failing her. Instead of satisfying Anna, all I do is make her more frustrated."

"That's not true," his wife protested. "I can still enjoy sex without coming."

I thought I saw a flicker of anger in Brian's eyes when Anna said that.

"Is it possible that it might have nothing to do with you," I asked him, "that it might be mostly Anna's problem?"

Brian gave me a grudging nod, but I could see that he was still angry and I think I knew what was upsetting him: He suspected that his wife was *deliberately* holding back on him. If she was not having orgasms, she was purposefully depriving *him* of satisfaction or worse, she did not love him enough. He could not get out from behind his preoccupation with his own performance to see that if Anna was depriving anyone of pleasure, it was *herself.* He had convinced himself that he was only concerned with Anna's sexual satisfaction; in reality, he was only concerned with his own performance.

Unhappily, husbands (and wives) with performance anxiety see every sexual encounter as a test—and a potential failure. And often they rig the test to make sure they fail. The test may just start with: "Can I do it [have an erection] at all?" But that is just the preliminary. Next comes: "Can I last long enough to make her come? To make her come before I do? To make us come at the same time?" The requirements for a passing performance keep getting upped to keep pace with our insecurities. I spoke with one performance-oriented man whose wife often enjoyed multiple orgasms. And he, of course, counted them. Thus, if she had four orgasms on one night and only three on a succeeding night, he got upset. Maybe he was doing it wrong!

There is an old Lenny Bruce routine in which he recalled listening through the wall to his brother making love to his girlfriend. All young Lenny could hear was what sounded to him like a strange voodoo chant: "Jacomyet, jacomyet, jacomyet, jacomyet . . ." It took him months to figure out that it was his brother repeatedly asking—nay, *badgering*—his girlfriend, "Did you come yet? Did you come yet?" The girlfriend was probably having a less-than-delightful time. Like so many partners of performance-oriented lovers, she was being made part of the test. The goal—orgasm—was everything. And the process —sensual pleasure—was merely the means to that goal.

I call these performance-oriented lovers Hard Workers. They work at sex the same way they work at most everything else in their lives: earnestly, proficiently, loyally, and with an eye on the goal. Sex is another job to be done well. The *doing of it* is nowhere near as important as the *getting it done*. It is simply another achievement. Obviously, there is little relaxed sensual pleasure for these Hard Workers. And there is frequently little relaxed sensual pleasure for their partners.

"It never feels like he is really there," one woman told me in private. "I feel like I'm some video game he's playing. Turning the knobs, pressing the levers, trying to get the highest score in the shortest time."

A frequent complaint of wives with Hard Worker husbands is that they are in too much of a hurry. Hard Workers usually do not want to linger very long with petting and foreplay, especially after they are already erect. They are afraid that if they are stimulated too long before they begin intercourse they will not last long enough to bring their wives to orgasm and that would be the greatest of disasters; for the Hard Worker to come before his partner does is his personal "failure." One sad irony here is that a great many wives do not really mind if their husbands have orgasm before they do. In fact, many would actually welcome it. The other irony is that if these men were not so preoccupied with lasting longer, they *would* last longer. Performance anxiety is the chief cause of premature ejaculation.

"It was great just to see him be spontaneous for a change," one woman told me, describing an evening when her husband had ejaculated while they were just fondling one another. "He was out of control for once. And I could just tell that it was the best orgasm he'd had in a long time. But then he started apologizing and making these guilty faces and all the fun was gone. He couldn't believe that I'd had a great time."

Nor could such a man believe that sex does not have to end the moment that he comes. Instead of apologizing, this man could have continued fondling his wife, perhaps bringing her to orgasm that way too. But this man was a Hard Worker and the curtain had dropped on his performance. No sensual lingering afterplay; the show was over.

It was a shame that he could not believe his wife; it might have been a marvelous relief for him, a great burden off his shoulders. Knowing that his wife truly did not mind if he came first, he might have taken the first step toward abandoning performance—and all the self-control that goes with it—and getting back to his own sexual enjoyment. Paradoxically, his wife would have started enjoying herself much more then too.

Another woman told me that her husband was so bent on "lasting forever" that she frequently faked orgasm "just to get the whole ordeal over with. Every time it's a marathon for him. How I long for a short sprint!"

For such couples I recommend the second touching exercise, where each partner *in turn* has an orgasm.

It is easy to resent a Hard Worker husband, but it is hard to get mad at him. After all, he *is* acting so selflessly. He is, it seems, doing all this hard work for his partner's benefit, for her pleasure. And in most cases, he does not perform with the macho swagger and obvious egoism of a Don Juan. Most Hard Workers go about the business of making love with all the earnest tenderness and attentive consideration that can be found in their counterpart, the Dutiful Wife. They are as busy "doing it right" as Boy Scouts working for merit badges. A Hard Worker seems to be all heart and solicitation: "Did you come yet?" "Was it good for you, darling?"

But is he really so selfless?

The Hard Worker is as preoccupied with control as any Don Juan—control of his partner and control of himself. He uses his partner to prove his own sexual adequacy. Her orgasms, first and foremost, are for him. Her pleasure is the means to his ego satisfaction, no matter how selflessly he goes about giving it to her. And his partner ultimately feels that. In the end, both partners lose contact with their own sexual feelings—feelings which begin *inside* themselves. And that is the real shame.

Excuse-Me Sex

"I know this sounds crazy," one woman told me, "but my husband is just *too* considerate in bed. Just when I'm starting to lose myself in my feelings, he'll say, 'Am I too heavy for you, darling? Does this hurt? Do you want me to slow down?' It's like we're at a formal ball instead of just balling. He's so polite I could scream."

I knew exactly what this woman meant. Hard Working husbands and Dutiful Wives can carry their "consideration" to the point where there is no spontaneous pleasure left for either of them. They are so focused on each other's responses that they have totally forgotten about their own feelings. Again, they are putting in a performance—a polite performance.

"For years, I only made love to my wife in the Missionary Position with most of my weight on my elbows," a middle-aged man confided to me. "I'd read in some marriage manual years ago that this was the right way to keep your weight off your wife and make it comfortable for her. It never occurred to me that she might enjoy it more another way."

Polite behavior in sex—what I call "Excuse-Me Sex"—takes the idea of "doing it right" to an absurd extreme. It brings etiquette into the one place where it should be totally forgotten: the bedroom. It took one couple several sessions before they came around to discussing something which was upsetting both of them: "After I have an orgasm," the husband said, "I usually just fall out. You know, it just comes out of her."

"Yes, what's the problem?" I asked.

"Well, she usually says, 'Ahh, I wanted to keep you inside me,' and I apologize and neither of us feels very good about it."

"But that's what happens with most people," I assured them. "The penis naturally recedes and it slips out."

Another husband asked me in private whether it was "right" to keep moving while his wife was having an orgasm.

"There's only one person who can answer that question for you," I told him, "your wife. I'm sure she wouldn't mind your asking her—but it probably would be best if you didn't ask her in the middle of making love."

The most frequent example of polite behavior in sex that I know of centers on the timing of orgasms—who comes first. And it is not just men who do the apologizing; many women end up saying they are sorry for "taking too long" to come. For some couples it becomes almost a comedy of manners, like two overly polite people trying to get through a door: "You come first"; "No, please, you come first"; and finally, "Excuse me, I came first."

It is enough to make anyone scream.

How to Look Like a Vogue Model While You're Having an Orgasm

One of the greatest disservices which frankly sexual movies have done is to give us an absurdly glamorous idea of how we should look in the midst of orgasm. No cringing. No contortions of the mouth. No rolling of eyes. No animallike groans and grimaces. We should all look as ecstatic and profoundly moved as Jane Fonda climaxing in *Coming Home* or as dreamy-eyed and romantically transported as Debra Winger in *An Officer and a Gentleman.*

It is remarkable how many women worry about how they look during this particular performance—their climactic performance. Time and again women have told me that they become inhibited just as they are approaching orgasm because they "lose control" and it makes them look ugly. They are afraid that their partner will reject them because they look unattractive while having an orgasm.

Orgasm, at its best, *is* a total loss of control. We grimace and groan, contort our faces, and thrash our heads in much the same way as we do when we give birth to a baby. And no, it does not look beautiful—not in a movie-star sense. But a great many men and women find something much better than mere glamor or attractiveness in seeing the expression of a purely natural and uninhibited orgasm. The sight and sounds of total abandonment can be a marvel to behold. We get to see one another in a state that we never otherwise see one another. And all the rest is acting.

Sex Without Performance

There are ways in which many of us want to keep some performance in our sex lives. Elements of seduction can add much-needed playfulness and even re-create the thrill and adventure of conquest. In Part II, we will see how deliberate performances can keep us from falling into tired and unimaginative sexual routines. But first, we must experience the ways in which the controls and self-consciousness of performance-oriented sex prevent us and our partners from taking pure pleasure from lovemaking. It begins, as always, with our basic sexual feelings and sensations. By getting back to these feelings, we get back to that point before performance begins.

For people preoccupied with performance, there is no better way to reconnect with these feelings than by doing *nothing at all.* A man who lies still while his wife touches and fondles him for once cannot control anything. No performance, no conquest —just his own sensual pleasure. It may be hard for him to be so passive—sex has always been something he did, something he made happen. But in the end, it takes a "Real Man" to simply receive sensual pleasure. He does not have to prove anything; he only has to enjoy himself.

6
Too Close for Comfort

A bright but very confused young woman, Tara M., came into my office and told me straightaway that she thought there was something "seriously wrong" with her sexually. She said that she was always turned on at the "wrong time."

"I'm just naturally perverse," Tara said, "and I can't seem to do anything about it."

She told me that over the past five years of her seven-year marriage she had gradually drifted into sexual boredom with her husband. It became more and more difficult for her to have an orgasm. Near the end, she said, she had only "given in" to his sexual pleadings about once every other month—"and then it was only because I felt so damned guilty." Finally, at her insistence, they separated; "I felt like I was drying up and wasting away," Tara said. "I decided that I would rather be lonely than feel like a sexless old prune at the age of thirty."

It was then that her "perversity" came into play: "David moved out and we didn't see each other for two weeks. Then he came by on a Saturday to pick up our daughter and when he brought her back and put her to bed, I asked him to stay for a drink. And while we sat there facing each other across the room, I found that I suddenly kept thinking about having sex with him. I couldn't help myself, so I told him and the next thing we knew we were in bed having the best sex we've had since before we got married."

Tara's story did not end there. Over the next six months,

whenever David came by on Saturdays, they made hot, uninhibited love in what had formerly been their marriage bed and
Tara had an orgasm each time. About this time they both
agreed that it was silly for them to continue living apart—since
a failing sex life had been the chief reason why they had separated—so David moved in again.

"The very first night he was back," Tara told me, "I just froze
up sexually. When he touched me, it felt like an attack. And
when he got on top of me, I felt like I was being closed into a box
—a coffin—it felt so claustrophobic. That's the way it's been
ever since. And yet I know that if he moved out, I'd get the hots
for him again. If that isn't perverse, I don't know what is!"

Tara's behavior may seem odd, but it is also all too common.
In one way or another many couples turn off sexually when they
feel they are getting "too close" to their partners; and once they
put some "distance" back into their relationship, they start to
feel turned on again. Without going to the extremes that Tara
and David had, many couples build a similar kind of distance
into their relationship to keep their sex lives from drifting into
apathy: They fight and then make up in bed; they spend periods
away from one another and then have passionate "homecom-
ings." Back and forth they go like toy magnets which can get
only so close and then "repel" one another. Sometimes it works
well—a couple find a balance of "proximity" and "space" which
they both can live with and which keeps both of them sexually
active. And sometimes the strain and uncertainty of having a
relationship which is constantly in flux takes its toll on one or
both of them and the marriage, like Tara and David's, reaches
an impasse.

But if the fear of being "too close" is one chief reason why we
end up feeling sexually turned off, its close rival is the frustration of "not feeling close enough." And this, not surprisingly,
turned out to be David's major frustration.

"I've always felt like Tara was pulling away from me when I
reached for her in bed, except for that time when we were
separated, of course," David told me. "It's like I could never
completely have her for my own. You've heard of having one
foot out the door—well, Tara always seems to have one foot out
of the bed."

David complained that he constantly felt lonely in his relationship with Tara, that she never seemed to totally give herself to him. "I never know how she is going to react to me from one day to another," he said. "And sometimes when I crawl into bed with her, she seems so isolated—so self-contained—that I feel like I'm crawling into bed with the Sphinx. And it's just too damned lonely to make love to a sphinx."

Tara and David were on the "Too Close/Too Distant" Sexual Seesaw: She could only make uninhibited love when she felt there was "breathing space" between them; and he could only make passionate love when he felt he was "finally penetrating her armor." Thus far in their relationship, the only balance which had worked for them was to live apart and make passionate love on Saturday nights.

"Did You Ever Get the Feeling That You Wanted to Go, but You Wanted to Stay, but You Wanted to Go . . ."

Tara and David were sexually isolated by their *war* over intimacy. Whenever David got too close to her, Tara felt suffocated; when he made love to her (after they were living together again), she felt like she was being shut into a box—"a coffin," she called it. She felt sexually claustrophobic. David, on the other hand, felt perpetually frustrated by never feeling "close enough" to Tara; she always seemed elusive to him, especially in bed (except during the period when they were separated). He felt sexually "shut out" and lonely. And, of course, the more David pushed for greater intimacy—"to penetrate her armor"—the more Tara retreated into herself and turned off sexually. The more she retreated, the more he pushed; the more he pushed, the more she retreated. In the end, they had polarized one another into positions where they could have no contact at all.

In most of our relationships, there are elements of Tara and David's. One partner is more the "pursuer"; the other is more the "pursued." One partner says that he or she wants to possess the other more, wants the other to reveal her or himself more, to be more "open"; the other partner wants more "space" and privacy, does not want to feel smothered or overwhelmed. Naturally, these feelings play themselves out in sex: One partner wants to "possess" the other sexually, wants his or her partner to be more "giving" and responsive, more open sexually. Usually, this pursuer is the one who initiates sex more frequently—and is turned down more frequently. And the other partner feels pestered sexually, always "under attack," and "under demand." He or she usually initiates sex less frequently, if at all, and often feels angry or guilty (or both) about having to fend off the other's sexual advances.

The spoken (and unspoken) dialogue between these two positions is almost diagrammatic:

One Partner Says	The Other Partner Says
"I need to feel closer to you."	"I need more space between us."
"I never get enough of you."	"I need to be by myself some of the time."
"I feel shut out by you."	"I feel attacked by you."
"You're too secretive."	"You're too prying."
"You aren't open—you hold your feelings inside."	"You expect too much of me—you don't respect my privacy."
"I feel lonely when I'm with you."	"I feel smothered when I'm with you."
"You seem like a stranger to me."	"I know you too well—you seem *too* familiar to me."

The dialogue continues in the bedroom:

One Partner Says	The Other Partner Says
"You're cold."	"You're too needy."
"You aren't loose enough sexually."	"You're so sexually self-indulgent."

One Partner Says	The Other Partner Says
"You're unresponsive."	"You're a pest and a bully."
"You're holding out on me."	"You don't respect my sexual feelings."
"If you loved me, you'd want to make love to me more often."	"If you loved me, you'd leave me alone until I was in the mood."
"You're sexually selfish."	"No, *you're* sexually selfish."

Elements of this dialogue are probably familiar to all of us. There may be some crossover: A woman, say, may feel that her husband is not sexually "open" or "loose" enough, but at the same time feel that he is too sexually aggressive and demanding —a sexual bully and pest. But essentially the dynamic remains the same.

The key to a relationship which works is a balance and flexibility of these roles—not polarization. In a mature relationship, we switch from "pursuer" to "pursued" from time to time; we give our partners "space" when it is needed and we give "closeness" when that is needed. And most importantly, we try not to *force* our partners to either give us more closeness or more space. A power-play attitude of force or demand is doomed to drive us away from one another, as it did with Tara and David.

Tara saw just about everything David did as a sign that he was getting too close—she felt suffocated just by living in the same house with him and she felt attacked every time he reached for her in bed. Like many young and early middle-aged people today, she suffered from an exaggerated fear of intimacy. And in Tara's case, as for so many of us, beneath her fear of being "too close" lay a basic fear of "feeling too much." As we gradually explored her feelings, Tara said this to me:

"When I finally forced David out of the house that time, I had the most peculiar reaction. For a day or two, yes, I did feel relieved—like I could breathe again. But then I started to get this horrible feeling that *he* had abandoned *me*. And I'd say to myself, 'I always knew he would leave me. It had to happen eventually.' I could really work myself up. Then, when he came by on Saturdays, I'd want him so badly—it's like I wanted David to prove to me that he still loved me by making passionate love to me."

For most of us, the fear of commitment is really our fear of loss. Like children afraid of being abandoned by our parents, we are afraid that if we become too involved, too "close" to our partners, we will surely lose them—and the whole world with them. By rejecting them, we deal with our terror of being rejected. By demanding "space," we deal with our fear of being abandoned. We are like the man who could only deal with his terror of heights by living on a mountaintop.

A corollary to our fear of losing our partner is our fear of losing ourselves. Tara told me that she felt if she "gave herself completely" to David, she would never get herself back. She would be totally overwhelmed by him—which is to say, she would be totally overwhelmed by her love for and dependency on him:

"When we made love on those Saturday nights," Tara told me, "I let go completely. The sky was the limit. I'd be all his. Sometimes I'd have three or four orgasms before we were through—each one more delicious and overwhelming than the last. But then, like clockwork, I'd finally feel *too overwhelmed*. Like if he stayed and we did this again the next night and the next, I'd become totally at his mercy—almost his slave. I'd feel weird—like a drug addict or something. And then, oh what a relief it would be when he left in the morning. I could be *sane* again."

Fundamentally, Tara was afraid of losing control of herself—a fear that almost always manifests itself in the bedroom. Totally yielding to her sexual feelings, she felt emotionally unbalanced —"weird." And indeed, like a drug addict, she was afraid of becoming "hooked" on David; she was afraid of becoming a totally dependent child again.

Both men and women are subject to the fear of "feeling too much" sexually and hence of losing control of themselves. But sex, at its best, *is* a loss of control—it is letting our sexual feelings take over and letting our sexual inhibitions vanish. Yet we are afraid that if we lose control, we will become little children again—dependent and foolish little children. It is the same fear which prevents us from crying—especially in front of one another.

This fear can exist at a purely physical level: One man who came to see me complained that he could never relax in bed; he always felt tight. He could function all right, he told me, but he never felt that he totally let go. He said his orgasms were never entirely satisfying—they never felt complete. I asked him if he could remember a time when he had totally let go; he said, yes, but it took him several weeks to remember—and admit—what had happened on one of those occasions when he had abandoned himself to his sexual feelings: "It was with my girlfriend in college, and right in the midst of my orgasm I—well, I farted. It just happened. And I was mortified. I think I started apologizing or something. I remember we broke up not long after that."

"But what happened was not unusual," I told him, "tightening your anal sphincter—and passing air—is a normal reflex response at the time of a powerful orgasm. I'm sure it was embarrassing, but in a way it was a compliment."

Grown-ups supposedly do not flatulate in bed, nor cry or moan—that is what infants do. Yet by inhibiting this response, this man was inhibiting his orgasms. Because of the risk of being a "foolish child," he was denying himself fulfilling sex.

In a similar way, many women I know never completely relax sexually because they are afraid of what they will do in the midst of orgasm—cry out, moan, become tearful, roll their eyes, or let go of bladder control. Again, these can all be part of "letting go," but the fear of losing control wins out: They deny themselves satisfying sex because they do not want to appear foolish or ugly—out-of-control children.

Tara had the particular fear that by losing control she would become sexually dependent on her husband. She would become "hooked"—a "sex maniac." At one level or another, many women harbor this fear—more women than men, I suspect, because girls are warned more strongly of the perils of "giving in" and "letting go." And a woman who grows up holding on to her sexual feelings begins to think that when she does let go, the whole "dam" will burst: She'll never be able to stop it. In myth, a young woman was said to be forever bonded to the man who took her virginity. "A woman never really gets over the first time," the myth goes. "She is hung up on him for the rest of her life." It is a convenient myth as far as men are concerned: If a woman believes it, it will be self-fulfilling—she will never even want to stray from the man who deflowered her. But I do not for one minute believe that this myth is true in itself: Most women I speak with remember the first time mostly as a painful and not particularly sexually arousing experience; they do not feel sexually "hung up" on their first lover at all. Yet the myth lingers in our minds and with it comes the idea that women have the potential to become "hung up" sexually on one man, that their sexual dependency will get out of control.

An extreme example of this fear—one that many women have confided in me—is the fear that we are, deep down, really nymphomaniacs. One happy result of feminism and the Sexual Revolution is that that absurd word—"nymphomania"—has virtually disappeared from common language. In its heyday, the word referred to women who were sexually insatiable—who wanted sex with anyone all the time, as compared to men who were *supposed* to want sex with anyone all of the time. But again, the burden of this idea still lingers with many women. Like Tara, they harbor the fear that if they really let go, they will become insatiable—hooked on sex.

Tara's fear of losing control played itself out in an impossible scenario: She could only turn on to David if she knew he was about to leave. It made it impossible to have a real marriage with him. Yet hers is not so uncommon a story: Frequently I hear about couples who leave their divorce proceedings together and go directly to the nearest bed.

But there are many of us who play out a similar scenario in a less extreme form: We play a continual game of brinkmanship with one another. We fight; one partner threatens to leave forever; and then, with one foot out the door, we fall into each other's arms—and into bed.

One woman told me, "Whenever we reach that point in a fight where one of us decides that the marriage is utterly hopeless, that there's no sense in going on, that's the point when we have the hottest sex. In fact, it's the only really good sex we have."

Fighting is often the strongest aphrodisiac in marriage. It gets rid of the bad feelings which have prevented us from approaching one another; it gets our juices going; and it establishes some "space" between us. Yet fighting which always ends in brinkmanship usually takes its toll: We eventually become emotionally exhausted by all the ups and downs and we long for some of the comfort and security which we sought in marriage in the first place; or we finally become bored with our own melodrama.

That is what happened to the woman I mentioned above. "The trouble is," she told me, "that over the years the routine started to wear thin. It was so predictable that it didn't work anymore. After a while, when he said, 'That's it—I'm leaving!' I'd think, 'No he isn't. In about three seconds he's going to smother me with kisses.' The whole business kind of lost its zing and then we were left without any good sex at all."

Without at least the threat of separation, sex was dull, just as it had been for Tara. When David came back to live with her, she felt turned off the moment he touched her. But, of course, Tara was turning herself off; it was the only way she could deal with the threat of intimacy. Tara's technique for turning herself off was the tried-and-true "bad list" method:

"As soon as David would get into bed with me, I'd automatically start thinking about all the things I don't like about him," Tara told me. "Big things and little things. That he smokes too much. That he's a lousy dancer. And physical things too: like the birthmark on his neck. I'd look right at it and get revolted. Of course on those Saturday nights, I used to be kissing him on the very same spot."

Tara needed to find a way she could sexually respond to David and live with him at the same time, but the only way she could do that was by establishing some "space"—and the control it afforded her—between them. If she was going to take one step toward David, he was going to have to take at least a half-step away from her.

The Loneliness of the Long-Distance Lover

"I never feel like I get enough of Tara," David told me. "She always seems removed, like she's holding back some important part of herself. She doesn't really share her feelings with me. And when we make love, I sometimes feel like I'm doing it all alone. Instead of a pas de deux, I'm out there doing a solo."

I hear complaints like David's almost every day, probably more frequently from women than from men. They speak of their intense loneliness with their mates, especially in bed. Typically, they talk about how it feels to make love to a "Silent Partner": "The minute he gets into bed, it's like he's struck dumb," one woman said to me. "He doesn't utter one word until it's all over and then it's something like 'That was great, honey. Good night.' And I feel like saying, 'Great for you, but lousy for me. All I feel is emptiness.'"

A Silent Partner is not only uncommunicative, he frequently closes his eyes as well as his mouth as soon as the sexual proceedings begin, and if he kisses his partner at all, it is once at the beginning and once at the end before his "parting" words.

"He's so self-absorbed, I don't feel like there is anyone really there," another woman told me. "He could be making it with anybody for all the real personal contact between us. For that matter, he could be masturbating with an inflatable doll."

Not only do these women feel lonely, they feel used—as if they are merely sexual objects, not persons. And missing for all of them—women and men—is the feeling that the other person cares.

"If he really loved me, he'd be there with me," they say. "If he really cared, he would want to talk to me."

Challenged by their wives or husbands, the Silent Partner usually has a whole catalog of counterarguments:

"I communicate in other ways," he or she might say. "I talk all day, but it is only when I get into bed that I can relax and communicate just by touching."

Or, along a similar line, he or she might argue:

"Talk is cheap. If you talk, you take the magic out of sex."
Or simply:

"I'm just not the verbal type. I never talk that much, why should I suddenly start in bed?"

Another line of defense goes like this:

"We know each other well enough by now so we don't have to talk. And you know how much I love you without having to tell you all the time."

Or finally, like Tara, he or she might simply say:

"I need my own space."

*   *   *

I can deeply sympathize with the loneliness of these wives and husbands of distant lovers. Because we see sex as the ultimate "shared experience," it can be the most isolating experience when we feel that our partner is not "there" for us. And making love night after night with a partner who is so preoccupied with "performance" that he virtually denies our existence can be the loneliest of experiences. Similarly, if, like David, we always feel our partner pulling away from us—physically or emotionally—we feel rejection as well as solitude.

But perhaps many of us also expect and demand an unreasonable amount of closeness from our partners. If, for example, we are married to someone who does not express his or her feelings easily in every aspect of life, it seems unfair to expect that person to suddenly become expressive in bed—unfair to our partner, but especially unfair to ourselves because we doom ourselves to always end up feeling lonely and cheated. And maybe many of us seek reassurances of closeness and commitment more than is necessary: Does your partner really have to profess love every time he or she crawls into bed with you? Look at the total picture of your lives together—doesn't that at least begin to answer your need for reassurance?

If we are particularly in need of closeness and contact, we have a tendency to blow incidents out of proportion. We see a week of our partner's remoteness as a picture of our whole relationship rather than considering that our partner is going through a bad or depressed period or simply a period when he needs his own space. We have to try to see our partners as separate people with moods and emotional schedules which have nothing to do with us instead of drowning in our own insecurity. Silence is not always rejection—usually it is just a personal need. We have to learn to leave the other person alone some of the time—to just let them be and to let them be themselves. And to do this, we have to let go of the idea that we can ultimately change our partner—that we have the power to either "fix" or "destroy" our partner's life. We cannot "fix" anyone but ourselves.

Most of my work is helping people to change themselves—to discover and rediscover their feelings and to express them; to find new ways of responding to one another—yet in the end, I believe that true intimacy is achieved by *simply being ourselves* with each other. And by letting our partners be themselves. This is true sexually as well as in every other part of our lives. If, say, our partner expresses him or herself with moans and tears at orgasm, take pleasure in that. And if our partner expresses him or herself with bated breath and closed eyes, take pleasure in that too—for that is who he is. Furthermore, it is a mistake always to demand of sex that it be the height of shared intimacy —it can be many other things too, including just the satisfaction of a simple bodily need. And those times when it is just a need, we do not have to feel lonely—we can just feel pleasure.

Still, that feeling of loneliness can persist.

David felt "shut out" by Tara, and for good reason: She would only be close to him if he was about to leave. But, as I eventually discovered, their relationship had not always been this way. As it turned out, David had played his part in pushing Tara away. From the very beginning of their relationship, he had *demanded* greater intimacy from her.

"I always had this idea that two people in love would somehow 'merge,' " David told me, "but I didn't feel that happening. In the middle of anything—dinner, in the car—I'd just turn and ask her what she was thinking about at that moment. Or I'd stop everything—even sex—and ask her to tell me exactly what she was feeling right now. Needless to say, Tara just clammed up when I did that."

Nothing can make us withdraw into ourselves more than a demand for closeness. *And unconsciously David knew that.* By demanding intimacy, he was actually dealing with *his own fear of intimacy*—he knew it would push her away. We discovered this when David finally made an admission of his own about those "wildly sexy" Saturday nights during his and Tara's separation:

"She was like a totally different woman those nights. She not only did things she had never done before, but she said things that she had never said to me before—and sometimes she not only said them, she screamed them! She'd say things like 'God, that feels terrific!' or, 'I feel like I'm floating on a cloud' or, 'I could just gobble you up alive.' It was marvelous—but when it was finally time for me to leave, I felt a little relieved. I felt like it was all *too much* for me in a way, like we couldn't keep this up, night after night, or I would become totally raw—I mean emotionally. When I got dressed and walked out the door, I felt free."

There is an old Bedouin proverb which goes: "Beware of what you desire, for you will surely get it." After demanding intimacy from Tara all those years, when David finally got it, he felt overwhelmed. It is a turnabout which I frequently see in therapy: The wife or husband who has to "pull" his partner into therapy is often the one who is ultimately more "closed." But until they reach that point, the demanders have been able to keep their partners at arm's length by pestering them for more closeness.

The "psychobabble" of post-sixties psychotherapies has unfortunately aided us in pulling this trick on ourselves and each other. By insisting that our partners "let it all hang out," we cover our own fear of intimacy with endless prattle about "how we *really* feel." In the end, we create a verbal wall of false intimacy which is harder to penetrate than clammed-up silence.

David, it seemed, needed some space of his own, just like Tara. Now they could both begin to come closer together by getting further apart, by consciously controlling and respecting the distance they both needed.

The Sexless Soulmates

Many of us grew up with the marriage ideal of being "Soulmates." We would find our "perfect match" and over the years achieve "total intimacy" with him or her.

"When I was a teenager," one woman, Alice K., told me, "I used to have this daydream about meeting a man who would understand me perfectly the moment I met him. He'd just know exactly how I felt about everything without having to ask; he'd be able to read my mind. And, of course, that would be the man I'd marry. Well, when I met Carl in college something very much like that did happen. We were both majoring in art history, both specializing in Pre-Raphaelite paintings. We both adored Indian food and Erik Satie and Nantucket—the list just went on and on. It was thrilling. We couldn't get over how lucky we were to find one another. I remember one time walking out of a Truffaut film together and we just looked at each other and smiled: We didn't have to say anything; we knew exactly how each other felt about it. I think it was that night that I knew I was going to marry Carl. We hadn't made love yet, but I guess I just assumed that that would be perfect too."

Sex turned out to be far from perfect for both Alice and Carl. From the start, Carl was reluctant sexually: He said he wanted to "save" sex until they got married because she was "special." It surprised Alice: Carl had had a great deal of sexual experience —mostly one-night stands—before he met her and he felt sex had never been a problem for him. "I figured if he loved me that much, sex would take care of itself," Alice told me.

It didn't, even after they married. And when I spoke with Carl, I began to understand why.

"Alice is my best friend," Carl said, "the best I've ever had. I feel incredibly close to her—closer than any of my friends feel to their wives. And coming from a close family, that means an awful lot to me. So I decided that it didn't matter if our sex life wasn't so hot—it was a trade-off. It was worth giving up great sex to have such a perfect mate. After all, sex at its best is just a

few minutes of pleasure now and then, and real intimacy is
forever."

Ultimately, however, intimacy without sex was not enough
for either of them. As with those famous literary Soulmates
Virginia and Leonard Woolf, sharing everything but sex led
Carl to seek sex outside of marriage. But that solution, as for
most of us, finally caused more pain than pleasure.

The Death of the Mystery Lover

In the case of Alice and Carl, it was Carl who felt the sexually
numbing effects of too much closeness, although at first he did
not realize this. But from the beginning he had given me clues
to his problem: He told me that he valued his closeness to Alice
because as an only child of a divorced mother, he had developed a very close relationship with his mother; thus it seemed
likely that he unconsciously saw intimacy as a species of Family
Love as opposed to Sexual Love. To him, feeling close to someone meant that he had to turn himself off to her as he had had to
do with his mother.

After several sessions, Carl admitted that there was something else which inhibited him with Alice: "We were a lot alike
to begin with, but over the years we became even more alike.
We molded each other into the images of ourselves—even physically. Like Alice will raise one eyebrow when she is making a
point—just like I do. That's a gesture she's acquired since we got
married. Sometimes when I look at her I feel like Narcissus
looking at himself in the pool. But I don't think I'm really Narcissus—I don't want to make love to myself. When I make love, I
want to be able to *forget myself.*"

Carl had put his finger on a major reason why too much
closeness can kill our sexual feelings in a relationship: It can kill
the fantasy component of our sexuality; it can kill the Mystery
Lover in all of us.

Part of the excitement Carl had felt in sex outside of marriage
—with someone "new"—was that *he was a stranger too.* The
person in bed with him did not have a complete idea of who he

was or how he felt about everything so Carl was free to be whomever he wanted to be—to be a Mystery Lover. He could express new feelings—not just those which Alice had already defined as the "real" Carl. He could indulge in a fantasy which not only included his lover, but himself too: He could forget himself and just make love.

At home, Alice and Carl were so focused on each other, so involved with their relationship, that it was difficult for them to focus on sex. After some time, Alice was able to admit that all this mutual involvement had a sexually inhibiting effect on her too: "Whenever we make love—or attempt to make love—I usually think about what Carl must be feeling. I try to get into his head— Is he feeling tense? Is he tired? Is the light too bright for him? Does he like the way my hair looks? And then when he actually touches me, it comes as a bit of a shock, like 'Hey! I forgot all about my own body.'"

Alice was so involved with Carl—with being a perfect Soulmate—that she had, indeed, forgotten about her own body and her own sexual feelings. Paradoxically she had turned off her sexual responses to Carl because she was so totally focused on him. And Carl had felt this too: He resented that she was sexually unresponsive to him; "Alice is so sweet," he said, "that she is cold."

Alice and Carl were so locked into intimacy that they had locked out sex. My task, as we will see later, was to help them become more of "strangers" to one another, to help them stop focusing so intently on each other so that they could start focusing on sex. Both of them had to learn how to be more selfish sexually so that they could become more sexually responsive to one another. By putting some distance between them, I was sure, they could come closer to one another—in bed.

Let the Sun Shine In

The end of sex signaled the end of Alice and Carl's relationship, just as it had signaled the end of Tara and David's. So sex seemed like a good place to begin with both couples.

To start, I suggested that we put the whole issue of "intimacy" on hold for a while. All the pushing and pulling for closeness and space had put an impossible pressure on their sex lives.

"Cease and desist," I told them. "Let's get your sex lives going again and the 'intimacy' will take care of itself. It will find its own level, its own balance."

I asked each couple to work out schedules of "time apart." For Tara, this meant a "night of her own" once a week—and that included that they sleep in separate bedrooms on that night. David opted for a monthly weekend camping with friends. Alice and Carl settled on a night out for each once a week. Furthermore, I urged them to try to be "alone together" more at home too. I particularly warned David to let Tara be if she seemed drawn into herself and silent.

"See what happens if you wait for her to talk first," I told him. "My guess is that she will come out of her shell more quickly than if you pester her."

To get their sex lives started again, my basic advice was simple: *Have impersonal sex for a while.*

For the Soulmates, Alice and Carl, this was particularly disturbing advice. Their whole relationship was founded on intimate personal contact, how could they have sex—that most intimate of personal encounters—that was impersonal?

"The whole idea does not feel right to me," Alice protested. " 'Impersonal sex' sounds cheap—like something you could do with anybody."

"Exactly," I told her. "I want you to have sex with Carl as if it were with 'anybody.' Forget about him completely and just focus on yourself."

For years, Alice had been so preoccupied with Carl's feelings, that she had neglected her own. For them to start having satisfactory sex, Alice had to feel sexual.

My first assignment to them was the basic touching exercise, with Carl—for the time being—doing all the touching. I asked Alice to just focus on her own sensations:

Close your eyes and just concentrate on your own feelings. Forget anybody else is there. Fight the urge to think about Carl and how he feels about what he is doing—if he is enjoying it; if he is bored. None of that matters for now. He'll have his own turn later. For now, imagine those are just hands touching you—anybody's hands.

Alice, as I suspected, was resistant the first night they tried the exercise. She wanted to stop after five minutes.

"I couldn't relax," she told me. "I just felt too—well, guilty."

I urged them to try again—and again. On the third try, it was a resounding success.

"I never felt more relaxed in my life," Alice told me cheerfully. "I just tingled. And the best part was—I don't know how this works, but when I opened my eyes after it was over and saw Carl there smiling, I actually felt closer to him than I can ever remember. And in a totally different way."

For Carl's part, it was a success too: "It was fun just playing with her body—nothing serious, not all that scrutiny and intensity."

When it was Carl's turn to be touched, that went well too—although they "cheated" and made love afterward. In the end, their bodies had established an intimacy which all the shared Soulmate experiences had never afforded them—it was the intimacy of giving and taking sensual pleasure. By starting with "impersonal sex," they had put the distance between them which was necessary for coming closer together.

For Tara and David, the place to begin was by letting Tara do all the sexual initiating for a while. She felt "attacked" when David touched her, so I told her to do all the touching for a while. David proved resistant the first time.

"I just automatically reached out for her," he told me. "I wanted to make contact with her."

"Let her make contact with you," I told him. "Forget about her for a while. Pretend you are somewhere else if it helps. In fact, both of you can pretend you are somewhere else; just leave your bodies in the bed."

For her part, Tara "performed" the touching exercises, but she said she never really got into it.

"It just gets boring after a while," she said. "I keep thinking of about a million other things I'd rather be doing."

"Like what?" I asked.

"Well, reading for one."

"Take a book with you next time," I told her. "You can read all you want while you're touching him."

The exercises went better after that, but the real breakthrough for them came after I offered another suggestion. Tara had given me a clue to what would work for her when she had asked for one night a week all her own—including sleeping in separate bedrooms.

"For a while," I told them, "make that night the only night you have sex. Even if Tara goes out, wait up for her, David, and make love when she comes home. And afterward, be sure to go off and sleep in separate beds."

They both laughed when I suggested this idea: They knew very well what I was driving at—to re-create the distance which had made those Saturday nights when they were separated so marvelous. But it worked. And as far as I know, it is still working for them.

"I still feel a little 'perverse,' " Tara told me at their last session. "But I'm also very happy."

7
The World's Most Competitive Indoor Sport

Last year when the Science Section of the New York *Times* reported on recent statistics showing that the average American couple makes love with decreasing frequency the longer they are married, I swear I could hear a citywide sigh of relief which echoed from the Battery to the Bronx.

Every couple seems to think that every *other* couple is "doing it" more frequently than they are—and probably "doing it" better and enjoying it more. Invariably, when I ask a couple how often they have sex, after answering they say, "Is that normal?" or, "Are we within the normal range?"

And I reply, "Normal for what? Your age? Your weight? Are you asking me if you are *average?* Are you average in everything else you do? Is that what you want to be?"

American couples are preoccupied with "keeping up their average." It seems every one of them has some absolute number in mind—be it once a day, once a week, or once a month—and if they fall behind, they start to feel like losers. There is something wrong with their sex life. They aren't "normal." And often they end up blaming one another for their "low average." The last question on these people's minds is whether they actually *desire* sex more frequently than they are having it. That somehow seems irrelevant. The "number" has a life of its own; it is all that counts. This preoccupation with a "normal average" makes couples equal partners in the most prevalent kind of Performance Sex—husband and wife become teammates in the world's most competitive indoor sport. Unfortunately, it is a sport in which everyone loses.

Keeping It Up with the Joneses

Sally and Ted M., an attractive New York couple in their late thirties, sat nervously in my office for several minutes before either of them was able to talk. Finally, after considerable prodding from me, Ted told me their "problem": "We're undersexed. On the average, we only make love once a month—and sometimes it can go up to six weeks."

"We feel like we're old before our time," Sally chimed in. "I think it's because we got a bad start. We got married right out of college in the sixties when everybody else was having sex all over the place. We just never got our engines going up to speed."

Again, they both fell silent. They were both conservatively dressed, well-groomed people who spoke quietly and deliberately.

"Do you feel frustrated much of the time?" I asked.

"Yes," Ted answered. "Especially when I realize that five or six weeks have gone by without our doing anything."

"I meant *sexually* frustrated," I said, "not *statistically.*" Both of them allowed themselves little smiles. Indeed, Ted's frustration at this point had more to do with an unfulfilled number than with his unfulfilled desire. His very first words belied his attitude: "Undersexed" clearly meant under the average, under what he considered to be normal. And Sally was obviously concerned with how they compared with other couples too: She was sure that in the sixties "everybody else was having sex all over the place." She was worried about how they compared— about missing out on something which everybody else had—not about what her true desires were.

As it turned out, both Ted and Sally did have greater appetites for sex than they had put into practice. But before they could get to their honest sexual feelings and needs, they had to get over comparing their sex lives with other couples'. In fact, by focusing on "statistics" they had been able to avoid facing the inhibitions which were keeping them from being more sexually expressive. They had come to me hoping that I could help them "up their average"—they wanted to learn how to *do* sex more frequently so they would be "normal." But my task was to get them to stop "doing" sex altogether and to start "having" sex—sex which begins with natural, uninhibited desire. The numbers, I told them, will take care of themselves.

Another couple who saw me had a competitive problem that would have seemed comical if they had not been so unhappy. Peg and Peter L., a professional couple in their early forties, were beside themselves with anxiety—and fatigue—when I first saw them. They knew exactly what their problem was: A year ago, a new couple had moved into the apartment next to theirs. Only a thin wall separated their bedrooms and every night Peg and Peter heard this couple make noisy love which seemed to last for hours. Not long after, Peg and Peter found that they were rarely making love themselves anymore.

Both Peg and Peter said that they thought their problem was "stupid," that they were ashamed of letting this "phantom" couple get to them in this way, but they also said that somehow it made them both feel insecure sexually, that it had touched a sore point which had been lurking under the surface of their relationship all along.

I told them that their problem was not unusual at all, that couples frequently fell into competition with other couples— real or imagined—and that it often had an inhibiting effect on their own sex lives. I said that their problem was just on a more exaggerated scale than most couples': Their competition was right behind the wall.

To start, I made the obvious suggestion that they should see if they could sound-insulate the wall—competition or not, noise can inhibit any of us from lovemaking or sleeping. That failing, I suggested that they move their bed into the living room or even find another apartment. But with this said, I then told Peg and Peter that they were right in thinking that this phantom couple had touched on a problem which had been lurking in their relationship all along: Becoming preoccupied with the phantom couple next door was a sign that they were not happy with themselves as sexual beings.

At the end of our first session, I gave Peg and Peter a paradoxical exercise to try. It is an exercise which any couple might benefit from—choosing their own "competitors."

Pretend you are the couple "next door" who are having sex more frequently and more enjoyably than you are. Talk about what you think they do with one another. Improvise. Try doing some of the things you imagine them doing with one another. Go with the fantasy as much as you are able.

It took Peg and Peter several weeks before they "found the time" to do this exercise, but in the meantime they had taken my advice and moved their bed into the living room. When they finally did try the exercise, they told me it was a total failure.

"It just made me more uptight than usual," Peter told me. "I felt ridiculously awkward. I can't pretend to be someone I'm not."

"That's wonderful!" I said. They both looked at me as if I had not heard him correctly. "I mean it. How can you be in competition with someone you can't and wouldn't want to be? That's really the point, isn't it? Sex is as much a part of who you are personally as anything else. It's an expression of yourself, just like the way you talk or sign your name. It wouldn't make sense to want your sex life to be like anyone else's."

Peter seemed to find this a happy and reassuring revelation, but Peg looked as if she were still not convinced. I asked her what she was thinking.

"It's just that there are still some ways I would like to be like other couples," she said. "When we tried talking about the couple next door, I realized that one thing they did was make more time for sex than we did and I wished we did that. Also they seemed to take their time with it more than we do and I wanted to try that too. Does that mean I'm still being competitive?"

"Probably not," I said. "Just now you've been talking about

what *you* really want, not about what you *should* want in order to be 'normal' or like someone else."

Again, as with most couples I see, I was able to start them on the sequence of touching exercises which reacquainted them with their own sexual feelings and with each other's bodies. It proved successful very quickly. Not long afterward—"Just as a joke," Peter said—they made love one night back in their old bedroom letting themselves be as noisy as possible.

"We thought it might be fun for the neighbors," Peg laughed.

Frequently we fall into sexual competition with a couple we know, members of our group of friends. Often, they are an attractive couple who take care in their dress and grooming and who always seem to be kissing and fondling one another. In some cases they may make coy allusions to how "hot" their sex life is. It is hard not to feel inadequate around such a couple— they do seem to be having more fun.

But are they?

Maybe it comes from years of being a therapist, but I am always suspicious of couples who make such a big show of their sexuality and their sex lives. Very simply, I suspect that it is a coverup for a failing sex life or it is a manifestation of the nervousness which frequently accompanies unfeeling Performance Sex.

Still, it would be only another form of competition to take comfort in my suspicion. What if in fact this other couple *is* "doing it" more or longer or whatever than you are? What can this possibly have to do with you and your own sex life? An unhappy—and unnecessary—result of such feelings of competition can be that we stop enjoying the company of this other couple. Like all forms of envy, this kind is not conducive to friendship.

The Swedish Sex Athletes Go to the Olympics

When I first arrived in this country from Sweden, I found that my fellow and sister countrymen enjoyed the reputation here for being sexual athletes. The very word "Swedish" connoted easy, frequent, and especially gymnastic sex. I can agree with this last idea at least: Swedes do tend to see sex as a gymnastic event; they treat it as a form of exercise—for "good health" and "vigor"—much as they regard sailing and skiing. In other words, I do not believe that Swedes in general have experienced their sexuality at a particularly personal or expressive level. But be that as it may, Swedes as *symbols* of sexual "champions" provide a good example of another way we become sexually competitive: We believe *whole groups* of people are "doing it" more and better than we are. But this kind of mythology cuts both ways.

We can find ourselves longing for a Swedish lover (or a black or Latin lover) to such an extent that we find our own sex lives— and our own husband or wife—sorely lacking. "I feel nothing in sex," people frequently tell me, to which I reply, "Nothing at all? Or less than you expect?" Our fantasies about mythical sex athletes, "voracious" and "indefatigable" lovers, make the reality of our own bedroom scenes seem like a cheat—second best. Why are the Swedes (or the men and women with Swedish lovers) having all the fun? *Why are blacks, Italians, teenagers, all of those who are single or divorced having more and better sex than we are?*

This common kind of jealous, competitive thinking—a sort of inverted prejudice—can only lead to bitterness and sexual dissatisfaction at home. And as far as I can tell, these myths are based on little, if any, truth. Yes, some of these groups I have mentioned may be more devoted to sex, but is theirs a devotion to sexual enjoyment or to sexual *performance?*

As I said, this mythology can cut both ways and a black man, for example, may feel he has quite a demanding reputation to live up to; the pressure to perform may always be with him. For a black man to temporarily fail sexually—to have, say, just a single night of sexual fatigue—may be enough to make him feel like a total failure.

The same pressure exists in various forms for each of these groups. Consider a single or recently divorced man in his thirties or forties: According to the myth, he is out there having sex all the time. His married friends are forever giving him sly

winks and prodding him for the details of his "swinging" life.
But it may only be their fantasy, not his reality, and he may find
himself trying to live up to their expectations because *he* is
competing with them too. It is a zero-sum game.

As one recently divorced man explained it to me, "I felt like a
real loser when my marriage broke up, but suddenly I realized
that a lot of my married buddies were envious of me. Every
time I took a woman out, they were sure I was doing all kinds of
crazy things with her. They had no idea how lonely I felt, how
much I envied them. So pretty soon I found myself taking out
sexy-looking women just to make them envy me. The fact is I
don't think any of us were having that much fun."

Today, the post–Sexual Revolution generation of teenagers is
the object of widespread jealousy and competition, especially
among middle-aged marrieds who came of age in a period of
greater sexual repression. Sometimes this envy turns to bitter
disapproval: We say that today's teenagers are dissolute and
soulless, wasting themselves in aimless promiscuity. We cite the
rise of teenage pregnancies and venereal disease with special,
smug satisfaction: It serves them right. But others of us are
outright jealous and feel shortchanged by history: We missed all
those lovely sexual adventures in the prime of our lives. It's not
fair. Why didn't we have what today's young people have?

Time and again I see couples who have let this particular
jealousy fester in their relationship, causing one or both of them
to become dissatisfied with their sex lives. They become preoccupied with missed opportunities.

"I missed the Sexual Revolution by about a minute," one
woman told me. "I was getting married when everybody else
was swinging from the chandeliers."

"I knew nothing when I got married," a man told me. "I was
totally sexually naive. And suddenly everybody was having fun
and I was tied down. No wonder I started sowing my wild oats
after I got married."

I would venture that the single greatest cause of divorce in
the past twenty years is our preoccupation with missed sexual
opportunities. We resented having to make love to just one
person while "everyone else" was out there swinging. We felt
cheated and so we began to cheat and in many cases this put an

intolerable strain on our marriages. Again, by focusing on missed opportunities and on the so-called swingers and "liberated" teenagers around us, we are avoiding the best sexual opportunity of our lives: building a solid, adventurous, and varied sex life with the one person we love.

All in the Family

Perhaps the most common form of competitive sex I encounter is intramural: Father with son or son-in-law; mother with daughter; even adult children with their parents.

A suburban couple in their late thirties, Jill and Larry F., came to see me with such a problem, although at the time neither of them was aware of its cause. Their problem was simple and basic, they told me: About a year ago, Larry had suddenly wanted to have sex four and five times a week—more than twice what he had ever wanted in their marriage before. Jill said that she could not keep up with him.

"Enough is enough," she said. "Anyway, it's got nothing to do with me."

"Who does it have to do with?" I asked, but both of them just shrugged.

I suspected that this was not just two people with different sexual appetites who were having trouble reaching a compromise; something else was at play here.

"Do you have children?" I asked.

Jill said that they had two, a daugher twelve and a "wonderful," little baby boy—"Our darling 'accident,'" she called him.

"The baby must take up a lot of your time," I said to Jill.

"*All* her time," Larry said.

"That probably doesn't leave much time for sex," I said.

It seemed I was right. Since the baby was born, Jill had frequently put off sex by saying she was too tired or she had interrupted sex play because she was distracted by sounds from the baby's bedroom. And the more she put Larry off, the more determined he became to have sex even more frequently than they had ever had before. They had polarized one another: Jill by her preoccupation with the baby to the exclusion of her husband; Larry by his jealousy of the attention the new baby was getting.

To help them depolarize one another, I gave them a paradoxical exercise:

> I told Jill that for one month she should have sex with her husband on demand, as frequently as he wanted. And I told Larry to "enjoy himself."

The first week, they did indeed make love five times. But the next week it was down to four. And the next two weeks and thereafter they were back to their usual twice-a-week frequency, what it had been before their baby boy's arrival. Faced with unlimited sexual opportunity, Larry had been forced to confront how much sex he really wanted, not how much he needed to "even the score."

It is not unusual for middle-aged men to suddenly want to be "High Scorers," to want to up their frequency from what it has been for years. It is a way for them to feel younger, to feel virile. The truth is, sex *can* have this effect if we come to it naturally; a middle-aged man who suddenly discovers his sexual potential and is able to put that potential into practice *will* feel younger and more vital. And in many cases, he will probably find that he has as much sexual energy as he did years ago. There certainly is nothing wrong with that. But a man who is focusing on sexual frequency as a number—a number which *symbolizes* how young and virile he still is—is doomed never to reach his sexual potential, because that potential begins and ends with his own sexual feelings.

At the end of their trial month, I asked Jill and Larry to try the basic touching exercises. Several weeks later, Larry said to me with a smile, "We're like that old cigarette ad. We're doing it less, but enjoying it more."

Fathers with teenage and young-adult daughters are particularly vulnerable to sexual competition. It's an old story: Daughter comes home with a young man and suddenly Dad becomes preoccupied with his own virility. It can take the form of High Scoring with his wife, depression, philandering with younger women, or, as I see frequently, sudden bouts of impotency. In one case I saw, a middle-aged man became impotent on the night of his daughter's wedding. The psychosexual reasons for this, of course, were complex, but I believe that basic sexual competition was at the center. "One generation passeth away and another generation cometh," it says in *Ecclesiastes*. It might have been a description of how this man saw his sexuality. The virility of his new son-in-law meant the death of his own virility. It was a competition he was doomed to lose so he gave up the game altogether.

Mothers are not immune from this competition either, although their jealousies often tend to take the form of a repressive attitude. It is not unusual for a teenage girl to come home flushed with sexual happiness only to find her mother waiting, ready to pick a fight about anything at all. A modern "liberated" mother might not berate her daughter for experimenting with sex, but that will not necessarily keep her from feeling the rage of jealousy: "Why is she having all the fun? I never did."

For most adults, sexual competition with our parents plays a small or nonexistent role in our sex lives. After all, from a very young age we prefer to imagine that our parents have hardly any sex life at all. But sons of philandering fathers are particularly susceptible to sexual competition with their fathers—and with everyone else. And—the famous exception which proves the rule—recently I saw a married woman in her mid-thirties who told me the following story with more than a trace of jealousy:

> I told my mother, who is almost sixty, about the new contraceptive sponges, the kind you can only use once. She asked me how much they cost and when I told her a dollar, she said, "My goodness. It's a good thing your father and I don't need them anymore. That could cost us almost $25 a month." God, she ruined my day!

But Who's Winning?

Of all the competitions we engage in—over money and power, territory and physical strength, popularity, status, achievement, and sports—sex is the only one where we can never really be sure who is winning. Joe may have a young and attractive wife, but are they really having more and better sex than we are? We are not privy to their bedroom, only to what Joe tells us. And we all know that everyone lies about sex—it began in the locker room and never stops. It's the safest lie there is: The only possible evidence is a pregnancy and that does not count anymore. But what makes this all especially peculiar is that with no reliable scorecard in the biggest of all competitions, most of us are still convinced we are losing.

But who *is* winning?

Somehow most of us have gotten stuck with the notion that we are the only people in the world who are holding back our sexuality, that we alone are repressed and inhibited from having more active sex lives while everyone else is "doing it all the time."

And if Joe's lies are not enough to confirm this suspicion, what we hear and see in the media is. How could anyone who watches television (just the commercials will do) or who goes to the movies and reads popular novels and magazines think anything else? In the world portrayed by the popular media everyone *is* "doing it more" and doing it "more skillfully," having more partners, lasting longer, and clearly enjoying it more than we are. And, of course, they are far better-looking, better sexually endowed in every way, giving rise to one of the most destructive myths of them all: that "beautiful people" have better sex than the rest of us.

The people we see on the screen and read about in novels are the only sexual competitors we ever know the "truth" about; it is only their bedrooms (and yachts and secluded lagoons) that we are privy to. In other words, the only sexual competitors we ever see "in action" are *fictional characters.*

But never mind. We are still convinced that we are "under-sexed" and "below average," losers in the Grand Sexual Sweep-stakes.

Poor Man's Bluff

It seems strange, indeed, that the most private of acts is the most public of competitions. But at one time in our civilization sexual competition had a very significant public correlative: The more children one produced (particularly boys), the more powerful and economically productive one's family was. Tribal chieftains and kings were judged by the number of children they fathered. Potency and fecundity really did equal competi-tive power. Rare, indeed, was the man of power who could not make babies.

Here, again, is an example of the way remnant behavior has lingered with us. Sexual potency and activity remain competi-tive in an era when having loads of children is usually an eco-nomic strain. Today, the upper classes most often confine them-selves to two or three children while it is the poor who are making babies; as a parody of an old song went, "The rich get richer and the poor get children." But "doing it" more and better, even in the era of contraception, remains a symbol of power. If this application of remnant behavior theory seems farfetched, consider this myth which is still very much with us: A man who fathers boys is still considered more of a "man" than the father of girls. We still see him as more "potent."

Through the ages, sexual activity became the poor man's bluff, the last arena where he could still win. Even if another man was richer or more powerful, if the poorer man was having more sex—or at least giving the impression that he was—then he, somehow, was the ultimate winner. (This was especially true, of course, if the poor man was having sex with the rich man's wife or mistress.) In life's overall competition, sex was the Great Equalizer.

There is no better example of this in America than the com-petitive rage which goes with the stereotype of the sexually

potent black man: while the Master was in the big house drinking bourbon, his black slave was out in the cabins making love
all night—and whites found it infuriating to the point of homi-
cidal rage. White men became—and some still remain—obsessed with the black man's sexuality, from the size of his penis
to his capacity for sexual endurance. And some black men still
take pride (as well as enduring tremendous performance pressure) in their reputation, allegedly seeing their ultimate
"achievement" as the seduction of a white woman.

Popularized Freudian psychology confirms this way of seeing
competition. This theory maintains that *all* competition is ultimately sexual, that the man or woman who seeks power in the
realm of, say, business is sublimating his or her sexual drive; he
or she is "really" after sexual power. This is, at best, an oversim-
plification of Freudian theory that only abets our preoccupation
with sexual competition. It justifies it as "natural" and helps us
remain trapped in a worldview which prevents us from simply
enjoying our sex lives.

Dudley Moore's Telescope

In *10*, a movie which for all its nudity contains more sexual
irony than sexual activity, Dudley Moore plays a middle-aged
man who spends a great deal of time staring through his telescope at the home of his swinging neighbor, a younger man who
hosts a perpetual orgy. Dudley is obsessed with all the sex going
on over there and he feels cheated by not being a part of it. But
meanwhile, in his own bedroom, he never seems up to making
love with the woman he loves. His chief sexual activity is peering through the telescope—sex at a distance; up close, he loses
sexual interest.

Dudley's telescope is a marvelous symbol of the way competitive sex does us in. By competing with real or imagined people,
"out there," by comparing our sexuality with mythical groups
and with statistical norms, we keep sex at a safe distance. We
never have to see that lover who is in bed with us as a real
person. By making sex a competitive sport, we never have to

deal with our personal sexual anxieties. Again, we have found a way for avoiding our fears of losing ourselves in sex and of being overcome by sexual feeling. By keeping our eye glued to the telescope, we never have to deal with personal sex.

But as *10* so comically illustrated, the price we ultimately pay for keeping sex at a competitive distance is that we never get around to truly enjoying it. In Dudley's case, for all his peering and chasing after the elusive *10* (the pneumatic Miss Bo Derek), he never actually got around to making love. The rest of us who have our eyes to the telescope may be making love, but we are undoubtedly enjoying it less.

Competitive sex, like all Performance Sex, keeps us away from our sexual feelings. We are constantly looking for results, trying to keep up our average, or becoming High Scorers, but we rarely *really look* at the sensual body right there next to us. And when we do look, we are dissatisfied. Sex with him or her does not begin to compare with sex "out there." We slip into sexual boredom and listlessness. And if our "average" slides, we get even more depressed, convinced that we should be "doing it" more to keep up with the Joneses, to be "normal." It is an endless cycle. And it is an unnecessary one.

If You Are Afraid of Heights, Don't Swing from the Chandelier

Alan L., a serious-looking man in his early thirties, came to see me alone to discuss his "flagging sex drive." For more than two months he had not had any sexual contact with his wife and he felt terrible about it.

"I've got this awful feeling that I'll never make love again," he said despondently.

I asked him what else had been going on in his life recently. At first, he said, "Nothing much, really," but later he told me that a few months before he had gotten a promotion at his office and that he was quite concerned about living up to his employer's expectations.

"It's not at all unusual to lose your sexual appetite when

you're upset about something else in your life," I assured him. "I'm sure it's not a permanent problem."

He did not seem convinced. I decided to try another tack.

"How old were you when you got married?" I asked.

"Twenty-six."

"And all those years before you got married you never let two months go by without having sex?"

Alan finally smiled. "Hell, I went whole years without it," he said.

"I bet it didn't worry you then the way it worries you now," I said. "And what's the difference? Are you a different person now? Is your sexual appetite any different?"

"The difference is that I have sexual obligations now," Alan answered seriously.

"Obligations? That doesn't sound very sexy to me," I said. "And who are these obligations to—your wife or to your monthly average?"

Alan had created his own sexual problem. Instead of allowing himself a period of well-justified sexual inactivity, he was worrying himself to a point where he could develop a very real sexual problem. He harbored an idea of marital sexual normalcy—*a number*—and he had convinced himself that there was something seriously wrong with him if he did not attain that number. In fact, when I met with his wife, she was more concerned with Alan's depression than with any temporary lapse of sexual frequency. It took the two of us to convince him of that.

The best sex we will ever have is sex which is an expression of who we are. To expect anything else, to force ourselves to emulate anyone else, is doomed to disappointment and depression. When a woman who was physically timid in every way in her daily life came to me complaining that she was not "wild enough" in bed, I said to her, "If you are afraid of heights, why would you want to swing from a chandelier?"

We make ourselves—and each other—quite miserable by trying to measure up to sexual ideals which have nothing to do with the sexuality we really feel. The way you make love is your personal signature. It reflects your entire personality, no one else's. We have talked about The Myth of Sexual Maturity, but to me genuine sexual maturity is the ability to say that you like your sexuality—your sexual desires and appetites—just the way they are. And that if you do not feel like a "swinger"—and I'm not sure who *really* does—that is fine: That is not who you happen to be. At the risk of sounding like Norman Vincent Peale, it takes guts to be happy with who you are—sexually as in every other way.

The same is true with the way we regard one another. To expect one's mate's sexuality to somehow be *radically* different from the rest of his or her behavior is to create an impossible demand and pressure on both of you. I have seen countless women with husbands who are orderly and efficient, who achieve goals as quickly as possible in every aspect of their lives, and yet these women complain that their husbands are too "efficient" in bed, that they do not linger on foreplay and they come too quickly. What did they expect? The irony is that most of these women say they married their husbands *because* of these very same traits—they wanted dependable, achieving husbands. Why were they now so disappointed because they were not "wild and crazy" lovers?

True, much of this book is designed to help all of us find ways to loosen up sexually, and to be sure, most "orderly" husbands have the potential to be much wilder and crazier without "becoming someone else." I am not saying, "You made your marital bed, now make love in it—for better or for worse." I am only saying you should remember that the person there in bed with you is the *same* person you enjoy for being who he or she is every place else. If you married "Julie Andrews," don't expect her to be "Bo Derek" in bed. Remember, as Dudley Moore finally did, you didn't really want to marry Bo Derek after all.

We can begin letting go of these impossible standards by no longer judging each and every lovemaking session we have. If we see our lovemaking in the context of our lives, we do not have to question ourselves (and each other) afterward:

"Was it as good as last time?"

"Last week?"

"The first time?"

"Was it as good as it could be?"

"Have we done it often enough?"

"Would it have been better with someone else?"

If we put each and every dinner we had under the same scrutiny—"Was it as good as last night's?"—we probably would never enjoy another meal again.

"I Did It My Way"

Personalities are complex things. I may have oversimplified above to make a point: We all know that no man is *just* "orderly and efficient," just as no woman is *just* "physically timid." We do different things in different ways and we behave differently in different contexts. The "orderly and efficient" husband may be aggressive and daring the minute he gets behind the wheel of his sports car. The "physically timid" woman may be "loose and un-self-conscious" on the dance floor. Sometimes, we can learn to switch our behavior in one context to another. And sometimes we can help one another accomplish this goal.

Here is a simple—and ofttimes amusing—exercise for achieving this aim which many couples have enjoyed. It is a nonthreatening—and nonjudgmental—way of communicating to each other how you would like to see each other express him or herself in bed:

Alternate saying to each other, "I wish you made love more like you (give an accurate example, e.g., "like you drive a car") and less like you (another accurate example, e.g., "like you do the taxes"). Keep going until either you are both giggling or you are ready to give it a try.

In this game, you are not asking each other to be another person, only to express an aspect of yourselves which you know is there.

As one woman said to me after she and her husband had tried this exercise, "Now I make love as wildly as I used to play tennis. And the funny thing is, now I play tennis the way I used to make love."

8
Resisting Temptation

A young woman, Megan L., whom I had recently begun seeing with her husband in therapy, called me and told me that she had to see me *alone* as soon as possible. When she came into my office a few days later, the rims of her eyes were red.

"I've been crying all morning," she told me.

"What's happened?"

"I made love to someone else!" she blurted out. "It simply happened, bang, like that. It's somebody at my office. He just looked at me at lunch and I knew it was going to happen. We went straight to a hotel room. That was last week. We've done it twice since then." She shook her head miserably. "How did I get into this whole mess?" she said.

"Why is it a mess?" I asked.

"Why? You know why?" Megan said. "I love Bob [her husband]. I want us to work things out. And now this happens!"

I looked at Megan. I could not help feeling sympathy for her distress, yet I was disappointed that she refused to take responsibility for her infidelity—just as all along she had refused to take responsibility for her sexuality in her marriage.

"You make it sound like it is all happening to someone else," I said to her.

Most people I see who have been unfaithful to their partners tell me that "it just happened." Like a teenage girl who loses her virginity by being "swept away" against her better judgment, they protest that they "could not help themselves" or that it was the drinks or the circumstances which caused their infidelity. But no matter how much they deny their responsibility for what "just happened," they are stuck with the consequences: confused feelings, guilt, and the fear of losing their spouses and family—*the whole mess.*

I certainly am not going to offer a moral lecture here on the "sin" of infidelity; that is not the business I am in. But I do think we are all obligated to ourselves as well as to our partners to examine the reasons *why* we are tempted to be unfaithful and to consciously decide *if it is worth it* to give in to these temptations. And yes, I guess I do have one moral premise: I don't think grown-ups should allow themselves to get away with saying, "It just happened."

Torn Between Two Lovers

Megan's dilemma, she told me, was that she was suddenly in love with two men at once: "Bob is my rock. He's my security, my best friend, the father of my son. I couldn't imagine life without him. But with Tom I feel things I've never felt with Bob —an excitement, a feeling of being alive. Sex is a totally different experience with him. I feel that if I gave up Tom, I'd be giving up everything that's young and vital in myself. . . . I feel horribly selfish, but I can't help wishing I could have both."

"In a way you can have both," I told her. "You can have both with Bob, if you are willing to try. That is exactly what we were beginning to work on before you gave up on your marriage."

"But I haven't given up on my marriage," Megan protested.

"I think you have—at least for now," I told her. "There's no way you are going to improve your sex life with Bob if you're making love to someone else too."

Megan protested again, although this time not so vehemently. She said that she knew other women who had told her that an affair had "spiced up" their married sex life.

"I'm sure these women made love more frequently with their husbands while they were having their affairs," I said. "That often happens. But it is invariably an expression of guilt, and guilty lovemaking rarely lasts for very long."

Megan shook her head unhappily.

In the two sessions I had seen Megan and her husband before this, they both complained of sexual infrequency and apathy. One of their chief problems, it seemed to me, was that they both felt suffocated by too much "intimacy"; Megan, especially, seemed sexually inhibited about making love to her "best friend." Theirs was a classic example of "Too Close For Comfort." I saw Megan's infidelity as an extension of this anxiety: By taking a lover, she was putting distance between her and her husband. But the question was, was it irreparable distance?

"You say that you are torn between two lovers," I said to Megan. "But what you have to ask yourself is, do you really love either of them? Or is this a way of not committing yourself to anyone at all?"

*   *   *

The reasons why partners are unfaithful—or are tempted to be unfaithful—are usually closely related to the reasons why they have difficulty expressing themselves—especially sexually —at home: The man who cannot verbally express his anger at his wife may act out his anger by having an affair with her best friend; the woman whose guilt about enjoying sexual pleasure when the children are anywhere in the house may "solve" her problem by having sex with someone else outside of the house; the man who cannot bring himself to talk to his wife about trying sexual variations may seek sexual release with a prostitute. The list of motives for infidelity goes on and on, paralleling the reasons we have explored so far in this book for why we turn ourselves off with our lifetime partners. And once we make the effort to explore these motives—difficult and anxiety-inducing as that effort may be—we usually discover that infidelity does not "just happen"; there is a reason why we make it happen.

Megan spoke of her attraction to Tom as an "obsession." All he had to do was look at her and she began to feel sexual, something which had never happened with her husband.

"There is some overwhelming electricity between us," she said. "I cannot deny that."

I am sure there was "electricity" between her and her lover, but I am also sure that not feeling close or committed to her lover was the primary source of that electricity. Further, Megan seemed to be "in love" with her obsession: Given the problems which had brought her and her husband into therapy in the first place, she found great relief in seeing her problems as beyond her "control"—that way, she did not have to work on her relationship with her husband.

All of us enjoy having a little "obsession" once in a while: As teenagers, nothing was more thrilling than "falling in love" with a movie or rock star. But when we act on these obsessions —especially after we are married—we run the risks which always come from mixing fantasy with reality. I have seen more than one case of men who divorced their wives and married their lovers only to have the same sexual inhibitions and frustrations once they were married to their new wives: Once the "fantasy lover" was a "real wife" the obsession (and the thrill) was gone and they were back where they started, but now with a broken family behind them.

"Hold it right there!" I can hear some of you protesting. *"Having an affair and getting a divorce are two different things. One does not necessarily have to lead to the other."*

No, one does not have to lead to the other, but the fact is, it frequently does. Somewhere in most divorce cases is a third party. He or she may not be the *cause* of the divorce, but that person often represents a critical step *away* from a marriage— from trying to make the marriage and married sex work. And once that step is taken, divorce becomes a real possibility. The question I asked Megan—and I ask any husband or wife who is embarking on an affair—is, "Were you ever a person to have casual sex? Or did you always—even *before* you were married— have sex in the context of a relationship?" If sex was always part of a relationship—as it was for Megan—an affair can mark the beginning of the end of a marriage.

None of this is to deny that many marriages do break up for good reasons. Nor is it to deny that second marriages to the third party involved in the breakup of the first marriage are often happy, sexually satisfying unions. One sad fact of life is that many of us do make hopeless mistakes in judgment when we marry—mistakes that no amount of therapy or dedication can rectify. I do not invariably say to every couple who come to see me, "You can work it out; stick to your commitment and sex will improve everything." There are many cases when that is simply not true: There may no longer be any *basis* for trust between the partners or they may have been hurt too much to ever forgive or they may have simply grown too far apart to ever be comfortable with one another again. Yet divorce, as we all know, is one of the most devastating experiences we can ever have, and to precipitate a divorce by "mistake"—by an affair that "just happens"—is a genuine tragedy. And it is a tragedy we would be foolish not to avoid.

I should also note here that rushing pell-mell into divorce court because *your partner* has been unfaithful can be a terrible mistake too. To be sure, infidelity is never easy to forgive and it is something you may never forget, yet by exploring your own temptations, you can at least begin to see your partner's mistakes in perspective—your partner's infidelities usually have more to do with his or her own inhibitions and fantasies than they have to do with you.

"I Do. . . . I Think"

Infidelity always raises the question of why we got married in the first place. And why we are still married. Megan easily admitted that the reasons she married Bob were still important to her: security, continuity, trust, someone with whom to build a family. She had had three long-term relationships before she married and, she said, "When the third one ended, I knew I couldn't go through this again. The whole idea of a relationship that I knew was eventually going to end started to seem meaningless to me. And when I met Bob, he felt the same way."

Megan was beginning to answer her own questions: If the reasons she had married Bob were still valid, why would she want to risk it for an impermanent affair?

Today, more than ever, people are coming to marriage with a history of sexual relationships behind them. For them, the deci-

sion to get married is a commitment to the security of perma-
nence after having experienced the insecurity of serial relationships or the emptiness of impersonal one-night stands. After
having had a variety of sexual partners, some people are anxious
about the prospect of making love to the same individual for the
rest of their lives; but they are convinced it is a far more desirable prospect than the opposite: making love to different people for the rest of their lives.

Occasionally, I speak to people who are an exception to this
trend: couples who came to marriage as virgins and now, living
in a world of "free sex," are preoccupied with the idea that they
have missed out on something. Many of these people are sorely
tempted to have extramarital affairs: They are convinced that
"everyone else" is having better sex than they are.

"It's like all I've had is vanilla ice cream," one young woman
told me. "It's natural to wonder what chocolate or pistachio is
like—at least just a taste."

"Why didn't you 'taste' them before you got married?" I
asked her.

The woman shrugged. "I was too uptight then," she said.

This woman, like Megan, had originally come to see me because she wanted help overcoming her sexual inhibitions and,
like Megan, she thought an affair would be a shortcut to this
goal.

"You can try all the lovers you want," I told her, "but it will
still be you in bed with all those different lovers—that won't
change. And what you really want, I think, is for *you* to be
'chocolate' and 'pistachio' and all the rest, and you probably
don't need another lover for that. That part is up to you."

But she was not convinced and did "taste" another lover,
although that experience, she admitted, did not begin to live up
to her fantasy of what it would be.

"It was a real fiasco," she told me later. "I was more nervous
than I am with my husband. I just lay there like I was a corpse."

Obsessions with trying other lovers all too frequently end up
in fiascos. The fantasy is usually so much sweeter and more
romantic than the reality. And the question remains, why are
we so willing to convince ourselves that sex with someone else is
something we *have to try?* Do we feel the same about other

experiences we have not tried—say, visiting India or becoming a Buddhist monk? I would not argue that making love with every person is the same experience—that certainly is not true either. But in the end, it is our *own sexual responses* which make the critical difference in the experience: Our "Dream Lover" may come along, but if we are uptight we still will not enjoy it.

I am certainly neither for nor against premarital sex. Coming to a committed relationship with sexual experience need not be the source of jealousy or mistrust it once was. But on the other hand, the current myth that we *need* to have sexual experience before we marry in order to "do it right" is a mistaken idea too. Married sex *is* different from noncommitted sex and the only way to "practice" married sex is together—in the marriage. A variety of sexual partners does not prepare us for marriage, only a commitment to making married sex exciting does.

"You Made Your Beds . . . Now Lie in Them"

A very confused and distraught middle-aged man, Jack L., told me the following story:

"I had been married to Barbara for ten years when I met Judy, and all those years I had never considered having an affair. Barbara was—and still is—a terrific wife and mother. But with Judy I discovered I had been missing something, a kind of intellectual rapport, common interests. We're both maritime lawyers, both interested in politics; we read the same magazines, talk the same language. I have none of that with Barbara. I found I really looked forward to my lunches with Judy and after a while it just seemed natural to complete the relationship and go to bed. Now I don't know what to do. Judy makes no demands on me; she never even suggests that I get divorced. And the fact is, I wouldn't want to. But I'm not sure how much longer I can keep up this double life."

I had heard similar stories many times before, stories of husbands and wives who realized they had outgrown their spouses when they met someone else who shared their interests, who "spoke the same language" they did. That part is always easy for me to understand. But it is the business of "completing the relationship" by sexually consummating it which always leads to confusion, to the guilt and torment of "lying in two beds."

Jack said that it had been "natural" for him to go to bed with Judy, yet if he had simply enjoyed the rapport he felt with her, the closeness, even the sexual attraction he felt for her, he would not have felt so divided, disloyal, and torn. Would his relationship with Judy really have been torturously incomplete if they had stopped short of going to bed?

Again, I am not making a moral judgment on Jack's behavior, but he had gotten himself into a situation which he found intolerable. He, like so many people who have affairs, wished he could undo it all.

Frequently, people argue that the ideal situation would be to have spouse and family in one part of their lives and exciting sex —with another partner—in another part of their lives. Yet this "ideal," appealing as it may be in theory, rarely works in practice: Most of us simply do not seem to be built to accommodate double lives. A recent case in point was the sixties and seventies experiments with "Open Marriage": A deal was struck between committed partners to allow—even encourage—sex with partners outside of the marriage. Nothing was hidden; it was all done in the spirit of openness and honesty. Yet one by one, these marriages faltered and finally broke apart. In the end, what seemed "natural" was to complete the committed relationship with a full and exciting sex life.

Tune in, Turn off, and Go Home

Megan, the woman who was "torn" between her husband and her lover, told me that she was sexually obsessed with her lover.

"I really wish I could free myself from him," she told me, "but I can't. I'm hooked on him."

"Maybe it is not as hard as you think," I said. "Most of us are past masters at turning ourselves off."

Megan gave me a reluctant smile. In my sessions with her and her husband before her affair began, we had discussed some of the ways they had been turning themselves off to each other over the years: The "bad lists" of each other's faults which automatically came to mind whenever they got into bed with each other; the ways they had focused on the "unattractive" aspects of each other's bodies whenever sex seemed imminent; the arguments, distractions, alibis, and excuses they used to avoid feeling turned on to one another. They, like most of us, had developed a variety of tricks and techniques to keep themselves turned off. I suggested to Megan that for once it might be appropriate to use these techniques: to turn herself off to her obsession for her lover, Tom.

"Next time you see Tom," I suggested, "focus on everything negative about him you can think of. So far, you've only been focusing on what is 'perfect' about him and what is far from perfect about your husband. See if you can switch things around."

Easier said than done, of course. But just the idea that her life could be within her own control gave Megan the opportunity to view her dilemma with a little perspective. It was not "magic" she was up against, it was herself. She began to seriously consider the idea that instead of spending a lifetime turning herself off to her husband, she could turn herself off to her lover and get down to her genuine priority: *turning herself on to her husband.*

One young married man I know told me his rather whimsical way for "resisting temptation":

"I am forever lusting after one woman or another. In the subway, in the office, just walking down the street, I find myself fantasizing about all the lovely ladies walking by. But then I play this game with myself called 'Shotgun Wedding.' I imagine that I am married to that gorgeous blonde standing in front of me: We have five kids, move to the suburbs, argue about money —all in the space of about a minute. And then, poof, I'm tired of her. I'm turned on, but I'd rather take that turn-on home to my wife."

Resisting the temptation to be unfaithful is not the impossible task many of us would like to think it is. We do not have to lose our sexual fantasies about other partners, just the consequences of acting them out.

Make Your Own Partner Your Dream Lover

As a sex therapist one gets accused of a great many things, but by far my favorite was when an exasperated husband called me "the Norman Vincent Peale of the bedroom."

I had just told this husband that if he took half the energy, effort, and time that he put into juggling his extramarital affairs and put that energy and effort into making his sex life with his wife more exciting, his life would be a lot happier.

If that sounds like Norman Vincent Peale, so be it. I happen to believe that it is true. I have seen too many people who find the time to schedule clandestine assignations with their lovers, but who have never thought of scheduling an afternoon or evening of sex with their own wives or husbands; people who carefully search out romantic settings for their extramarital encounters, but who never consider taking their marital sex lives out of their bedrooms at home and into a new and stimulating setting; people who find the energy to make love all night with their lovers but who complain they are always too tired for sex at home; people who can get themselves in the mood for sex at a moment's notice with a lover, but who wait for the "perfect mood" to strike to make love at home; people who will try all kinds of "crazy" things in bed with a secret lover, but who claim they feel shy or self-conscious about doing anything other than the "Real Thing" in their own bedroom. In short, people who make extramarital sex fun, but who insist that sex at home must be "serious" business.

The fact is, if we refocus our sexual energies in these and other ways—if we "think positively" about sex with our committed partners—I am convinced we can have the best of both worlds: the security and trust of a continuous relationship and the thrill and adventure of an affair—an "affair" with our husband or wife. Every one of us can make our partners into our

"Dream Lovers." Over the years, I have seen countless couples do just that and I know it is the key to a thriving marriage.

In Part I of this book we have explored the major ways many of us automatically turn ourselves off in marriage; in Part II we will see how we can turn ourselves on in marriage:

Instead of succumbing to "The Turnoffs of Everyday Married Life," we can try "Sexing Out" and "Naughty but Nice" Sex—*with our partners.* ,

Instead of waiting interminably for both partners to "be in the mood for love," we can try "Taking a Sandwich—and Each Other—to Bed" once a week and see how the "perfect mood" was waiting for us all the time.

Instead of stereotyping each other as sexless "Mommies" and "Daddies," we can try "Thinking Sexually" about each other all over again.

Instead of being stuck with serious "Real Thing" Sex night after night, we can try a whole "Sexual Smorgasbord" of variations with each other.

Instead of becoming preoccupied with the sexual performer's "Job of Sex," we can learn how to "selfishly" focus on our own pleasure with "The Art of Using Each Other."

Instead of suffocating sex by being "Too Close for Comfort," we can try making our partners into "Fantasy Lovers."

Instead of always seeing our sex lives as inadequate by involving ourselves in "The World's Most Competitive Indoor Sport," we can rediscover the newness of sex by doing it for "The First Time—Again."

In Part I, we saw how familiarity can breed sexual boredom; in Part II we will see how familiarity with one partner can breed sexual trust and relaxation: the keys to an exciting and evolving sex life. Like tennis partners who develop their skills together over years, who know each other's moves and responses instinctively, lovers can keep getting better and better by making love to the same person for the rest of their lives. In fact, they can have the best sex there is.

PART II
How to Turn Ourselves On

9
Thinking Sexually

There is hardly a man who does not fondly remember his adolescent days when the merest suggestion of sex could send the blood rushing to his groin and make an embarrassing bulge appear in his pants. Anything could set him off: the outline of a bra strap showing through the blouse of the girl who sat in front of him in French class; a fraction of a second of bare thigh as a young woman in a skirt mounted her bicycle; a movie poster of Janet Leigh in a swimsuit; and *dancing*—Oh, Lord, dancing did it every time.

"Starting in about eighth grade," one man told me, "the number one topic of discussion with the boys was what did you do with your erection—'boner' we called it then—when you were dancing close with a girl? The general consensus was that you were supposed to pull back your pelvis and stick out your rear so that the girl couldn't tell you were excited. Of course, that made dancing difficult—you always felt like you were about to fall over."

Memories of this sort do not come back quite so easily to some women: They were usually better schooled from an early age in denying their sexual feelings and they do not have a physical correlative to these feelings which is quite so obvious to themselves (or anyone else) as a bulge in the pants. Yet the sexual feelings were there along with the natural physical responses—what woman does not recall undressing after attending a high school basketball game and discovering that her panties were damp? An adolescent girl's sexual feelings were triggered as easily as any adolescent boy's: by a clandestine reading of *Lady Chatterly's Lover;* a bumpy ride in the backseat of a bus; just the sight of the word "sex" in print; and, yes, *dancing.*

After repressing sex as a preteen the sudden discovery of sex as a teenager was a marvelous surprise: "I remember having this astounding thought that everybody in the whole world only existed because somewhere at some time two people had had sex together," one woman told me. "It was mind-boggling. I would look at a crowd in the street and think, 'That's five hundred sexual intercourses right there!' "

A man I know confessed a similar "astounding" adolescent revelation: "I just couldn't get over the fact that underneath their clothing *everybody* had sexual organs. Everybody!"

Sex seemed to be everywhere when we were young. It bloomed bright and luxuriant like wildflowers in the most unlikely places. A curtain drawn across a bedroom window as we wandered by elicited an instant fantasy of tempestuous lovers' naked bodies undulating on the bed behind those curtains. A lone car in a motel parking lot in the middle of the afternoon set off an inevitable train of thought about clandestine passion. Mentally undressing strangers was an endlessly satisfying pastime. *Thinking sexually was a reflex.*

But somewhere along the line—often around the time we got married—we lost that reflex. It was buried in the countless new reflexes we adopted for turning ourselves off.

Turning ourselves back on begins in the same way it did in adolescence: by thinking sexually. By seeing the whole world and everyone in it as sexual beings with sexual feelings. And by catching ourselves before we automatically turn ourselves off to all this sexual wonder.

The best way to start feeling more sexual at home is to allow ourselves to start feeling more sexual every moment of the day. It is virtually impossible to keep our sexual responses under strict control all day long and then suddenly to switch gears the moment we are alone with our mates at eleven o'clock and be ready for passionate sex. We have to begin by resensitizing ourselves to sex, by letting our sexual fantasies play out without stopping them out of guilt or embarrassment. By letting our

1988

Tethercat

gaze wander uninhibitedly, abetted by our imagination, into the realm of sexual possibilities. And by feeling our natural sexual responses to this world—the quickening of our pulse, the stirrings in our groin, the dampness in our pants—as a source of pleasure, rather than aborting these feelings before they really begin out of shame or fear of "distraction" or terror of becoming a "sex nut."

"You must be kidding!" I can hear that voice of protest arguing. *"It's all one can do Not to think sexually all day long in the world we live in today. We are bombarded with blatant sex and sexual innuendos every minute—in ads, magazines, TV, movies. Sex is constantly blaring at us. And that's not even to mention the sexual blatancy of the way people dress now—You don't even need your imagination to think sexually today."*

Ah, but you do! Sex is not simply an object out there in the world. It is a response to the world. We can stand in the middle of an orgy and not have one sexual thought or feeling at all. In fact, I believe that all that sexual blatancy which bombards us from the media and in the streets only serves to *turn us off more* in the long run. It ups the ante of our need for "nonsexual survival." Like a city dweller who adjusts to an overbearing noise level by automatically raising his sound threshold—turning down his sensitivity to all noise—many adults have responded to the high-level sexual stimulants in today's world by raising their "sex threshold"—turning off their sensitivity to all sex. The result, I think, is more sexual numbness than ever. It is anything but a case of people *thinking sexually* all of the time.

"I Was a Teenage Sex Nut"

At a recent meeting of hospital residents, the question came up of whether or not there was any sexual activity among the patients on the wards.

"Absolutely not," one earnest young resident said immediately. "These are sick people. Sex is the last thing on their minds."

"Oh boy, is there ever!" another resident piped up. "When

the lights go out, there's always someone scrambling from one bed to another."

The first resident had turned herself off to the realm of sexual possibilities. To her, it was an outrageous thought that her patients had sexual feelings and needs. In all likelihood, this worldview was not just limited to the wards; she probably had difficulty imagining much of the general population as sexual beings.

Some people I know have trouble imagining that anyone over sixty is sexual. I have spoken with others who cannot really believe that anyone who wears a coat and tie and works on Wall Street has strong sexual feelings. And most of us, in our heart of hearts, find it difficult to accept the fact that our parents made—and continue to make—love.

But they all have sexual feelings—all of them. And it is good to remind yourself of that, to be aware of it as much as possible. It is sexually invigorating to recapture that sense of awe which that teenage girl felt when she realized that everyone in the world is the product of a sexual act and that of the teenage boy who realized that underneath everybody's clothing were sexual organs. To start thinking sexually again, we have to regress to this teenage frame of mind, this sense of wonder, this sexual giddiness.

"Impossible!" (That voice of protest again.) *"If I start to think like a teenager, all I'll think about will be sex. I won't think about anything else. And who's got time for that but a real teenager?"*

Nonsense. Time is not the problem: We spend hours every day daydreaming about money and career and mulling over the same problems again and again. Our real fear, I suspect, is that if we think like a teenager, we will come to behave like "teenage sex nuts." We will become "degenerates," obsessed by sex— hooked on it—and all we will want to do is have sex to the exclusion of everything else. We will never be able to concentrate on the "important" things in life again, so preoccupied with sex will we become. This may sound like an exaggeration, but many of us do carry the "teenage sex nut" fear around inside of us. We have held back our sexual perceptions and feelings for so long that we feel that just the slightest crack in the "dam" will drown us in our own sexuality. Our basic fear of thinking like a teenager, then, is that we will become sexually excited.

But that is the whole idea.

Sexual excitement does not have to lead to sex all the time—and certainly not immediately. It can be an invigorating, sensitizing pleasure in itself. (The fact is, teenagers do *not* have sex all the time, despite popular opinion—and anxiety—to the contrary.) We do not go "sexually berserk" just by turning ourselves on with sexual thoughts and perceptions and fantasies. We have plenty of control over ourselves—that is not the problem. The problem is letting go of some of that control.

Going Wild—in Very Small Steps

All right, let's regress. Not *every* minute of the day but here and there, let us switch the *focus* of our perceptions to the sexuality in our everyday world:

- Next time you pass a bedroom window with the curtains drawn, imagine what could be happening behind them—what very well *might be* happening behind them. Dream awhile. Let the fantasy wander on its own. And don't let yourself be stopped by your "automatic turnoff" if you begin to feel aroused. Believe me, you won't go "berserk." And no one has to know what you are thinking.
- Rediscover the lost art of "mentally undressing" people—strangers as well as people you know. Imagine what they *really* look like underneath all that cloth—their chests and bosoms, their bellies and buttocks, their sex organs. It is all there, you know. The only "illusion" or "distortion" is to think that they *don't* have bodies underneath their clothes. And remember, none of this makes you a "dirty old man" or a "nymphomaniac." Nothing could be more natural. Humans started mentally undressing one another from the day they started covering themselves.

· Imagine other couples making love—any couple. A couple you know, the couple with their arms around one another standing ahead of you in line, your parents, the Queen and her Consort. They all do it, you know. And it is not disgusting to them—at least not to most of them. Imagine what turns them on to each other, how they touch one another, how they feel. Again, let your fantasy wander on its own. You won't get in trouble. You won't get arrested for "indecent exposure" of your mind!

· *Most importantly,* don't become alarmed when you begin to feel sexually aroused doing these or any other exercises you may think of. That "alarm" is the way you turn yourself off. *Focus* on your arousal. Feel your pulse quicken, the tingling in your belly and groin, the swelling of your penis or the lubrication in your vagina, the sudden sensitivity of your entire body. They are all part of you, all natural responses. If we never turned ourselves off, we would go happily through a day becoming sexually aroused from time to time, fading into another focus, becoming aroused again, all as natural as laughing when something strikes us as funny and getting on with our business when the joke is over.

Thinking sexually is a frame of mind, a focus. I have prescribed a few exercises here for slipping into that frame of mind, but I cannot presume to write scenarios for your imagination. The fantasies are your own. Enjoy them.

"Excuse Me—You Might Turn Me On"

The anthropologist Desmond Morris has a theory that the reason we say "Excuse me" when we make accidental physical contact with a stranger is we are trying to blot out the sexual feelings and messages we are giving him or her. In effect, we are saying, "Excuse me—you might turn me on. And me, you."

When we were young and single, the slightest, most casual

physical contact with anyone could make us tingle with sexual excitement. And that feeling could remain with us for minutes, even longer, giving us a lift—a "high"—which seemed to make the whole world more inviting. No harm was done when a stranger's thigh accidentally pressed against our own as the bus took a sharp turn. It was an innocent source of pleasure until— "Excuse me"—we began to turn ourselves off in alarm.

"Hold it right there!" (That voice of protest again.) *"I hope you aren't going to suggest these 'accidental' physical contacts with strangers as a way of life. There are mashers out there— everywhere these days. I'm certainly not going to be a willing victim to one of those creeps."*

Sadly, there are more mashers out there than ever before. Even the once-innocent and harmless pleasure of "eye flirta- tion" on a bus or train—a favorite pastime on the bus ride into Stockholm when I was a student—is a risk these days: Too many men (and women too) take it as a direct invitation rather than a game with a beginning and end (the end of the bus ride). But that said, there *is* a distinction between being accosted by a masher and casual, accidental physical contact. And there is a distinction between *being* a masher and simply enjoying the pressure of a stranger's body against our own when we are pressed together in a crowded elevator. We know the differ- ence. We do not have to be either victims or mashers to allow ourselves this pleasure, this innocent turn-on in our daily lives. And, God forbid, should we make an error in judgment and some stranger does press us—and his luck—too far, this should not prevent us from getting angry and doing what is necessary to stop him. But on the other hand, we do not have to turn ourselves off every minute because of this possibility.

Consider the following situation: You are on a couch in your dentist's waiting room. Another person sits down and suddenly you find your thigh touching his or hers. Your automatic re- sponse is probably to yank your leg away. But what if—just this time—you did not. Instead, your head still buried in your maga- zine, you focus on the pressure of this strange body against your own. There is no doubt—this is exciting. Your leg feels warm and that warmth spreads to the inside of your thighs. You begin to have a sexual fantasy, not necessarily about the stranger, but anyone—real or simply imagined. If you are a man and begin to feel your penis stir, you simply rearrange your newspaper to cover any possible embarrassment. If you are a woman and begin to feel some dampness between your legs, you need not worry—no one has any idea. A little later, the stranger leaves and it is all over.

Now what harm has been done by this little interlude? You did not go berserk and commit a sex crime. You did not suddenly slip into the category of "degenerate"—a "dirty old man" or a "nymphomaniac." You have not committed a flagrant act of disloyalty or infidelity toward your mate: You are, after all, fully clothed and this is basically just a fantasy. You are not obsessed or possessed. In fact, as the fantasy drifts away, you simply go back to your article about trade deficits or the Mets. But the fact is, you do feel more *alive*, more sensitive and sensitized for allowing yourself this small pleasure—and the pleasure will stay with you for the rest of the day, especially when you go home.

I am hardly advocating promiscuity here, or wanton self-indulgence. I am only suggesting that instead of pulling away, tightening up, and turning off every time we catch a stranger's eye or brush against someone passing through a door, we allow our *natural* responses to have their day. The world will not come tumbling down.

Bringing It All Back Home

There is probably no better place for thinking and feeling sexual than a party. It offers people groomed and dressed at their best. It offers physical contact through dancing. It offers an opportunity for flirtation. But it also offers the danger of hurting or humiliating our mates.

First, the danger. This has its appeal too: The Forbidden Game of dancing cheek-to-cheek with someone else, knowing that your mate is somewhere in the room. But, as you know, this can be terribly destructive, especially if you do not have a truly trusting relationship with your mate or if you are going through a particularly low sexual period with him or her. In this case, it pays to be cautious: The hurt is not worth the fun. Yet over the years many couples work out a tacit "flirtation quota" between them: the rules of the game. You know how far you can go—how close to dance, how much time to spend in intense conversation with another person—without embarrassing or humiliating your mate. And you also are aware that a little jealousy keeps you appreciating one another. If you know each other well enough, this need not be a problem.

But this said, there is another problem: Allowing ourselves the sexual pleasure of flirtation. Too often, dancing with an attractive man or woman who is not our mate, we automatically —and guiltily—turn ourselves off. "Yes, I'm dancing with some-one else," we seem to say to ourselves, "but I'm not going to *feel* anything. That would be going too far."

Too far for whom? Dancing is dancing—if your mate is not hurt by that, he or she will certainly not be hurt by what you *feel* while you are doing it. But there is something else which often troubles us: We feel that if we become sexually aroused by someone, we *have to follow through*—do something about it. Again, nonsense. Sexual arousal is a pleasure in itself; it does not have to go anywhere from there. There are no obligations, no "uncontrollable" drives. Dancing and flirting, we can feel our-selves as sexual beings—feel witty and attractive—and we can feel our bodies flush and tingle with excitement. There is no harm in that; no one has been hurt or cheated. And later, when we go home with our mate, we can bring this excitement with us. Instead of arriving at our bed after an evening of turning ourselves off, we arrive there thinking and feeling sexual.

And there is something else you can bring home: A fresh perception of your mate. As we have seen, the numbness of daily routine often prevents us from seeing our mates as any-thing more than vague presences. He can shave off his mous-tache and we do not notice it for weeks. She can come home in a new dress and it does not register. But at a party, we have the opportunity to see our partners as others see them. And that can go a long way in getting us to *think sexually about our partner again.*

There is an exercise which I often recommend to people who see their mates too automatically—and who thus no longer see them as sexual or sexy. One of my patients gave this exercise the monicker "Seeing Your Mate from Somebody Else's Pants":

> At a social gathering, watch other men or women relating to your mate. Imagine yourself seeing him or her as they do. Feel their attraction as they look in your mate's eyes, touch his or her arm, laugh at his or her stories. Fantasize flirting with your mate, "picking him or her up." Carry these feelings home with you that night.

Sexual arousal does not have to begin *and* end at home. If we persist in letting the automatic turnoffs of everyday life rule us, we cannot expect ourselves to suddenly start thinking and acting sexually during those few hours when we are alone with our mates. The human psyche—and body—simply does not work that way. It is a little like expecting a professional singer to give an impassioned recital after not having one musical thought or doing one scale all day. We need freedom to fantasize and freedom to "practice" our sexuality all day if we are to be sexual at home. As one woman whom I had helped to start "thinking sexually" again put it, "For a long time, I looked at the world with 'blinders' on—blotting out every sexual thought or sensation I had. I felt I had to 'save' it all for when I was with my husband. But after a while, there was nothing for me to save. Sure, all this sexy thinking is adolescent. But I'd rather feel adolescent *and* sexual than not feel anything at all."

they had to renew their sexual energy—and to do that they had
to renew their general physical energy. They may have been
using "fatigue" and "age" as excuses to avoid sex because of
anxieties we had not yet uncovered; still, to even start feeling
sexual, they had to start feeling more alive. As it happened, I
knew a conference would prevent me from seeing this couple
for two weeks, so the only exercise I gave them was this:

> Instead of watching television for the next two weeks, take a
> brisk walk every evening—no dawdling or stopping to smoke
> along the way. Try to get your walk up to a half hour before I
> see you next time.

Larry grumbled something about how it would be cheaper to
go to Jack La Lanne's than to a therapist if this was all I had to
offer them, but nonetheless he promised to follow my advice.

Two weeks later, when they marched into my office, Marcia
immediately announced that they were "cured."

"We've made love more in the last two weeks than we did in
the last half year," Larry said.

"Tell me about it."

"Well, after our fourth evening of walking, we both came
home exhausted and sweaty, panting like little dogs, and we
both needed showers. Marcia wanted to go first, so I got undressed and waited in the bathroom for her to finish. Then she
called out for me to do her back, so I just got into the shower
with her and did her back; then she did mine, and while she was
at it, soaped up the rest of me too. Well, one thing led to another
—you get the idea. The next night, we just both got into the
shower at the same time and the same thing happened. And this
last week, about halfway through our walk we'd both start up-
ping our pace in a hurry to get home . . . and to the shower!"

Larry and Marcia were indeed "cured." Unlike many other
couples I have seen who used the excuse that they were "too
tired for sex" as a coverup for avoiding their sexual anxieties
and tensions, Larry and Marcia *really were* too tired for sex—
just as they were too tired for almost anything other than
slouching in front of the television set. As it turned out, those
walks—and the showers which followed them—were the best

10

"Let's Get Physical"

Surely the shortest course of therapy I ever gave was to a couple in their mid-forties, Marcia and Larry M., who came to see me because their sex life, once quite active, had diminished in frequency to once every other month, and even then, they agreed, it was "lackluster and lackadaisical." From the moment they walked into my office—slouched in, rather—and jointly lit up cigarettes, I could see that this was a couple who had allowed themselves to become physical wrecks: They were overweight, short of breath, had poor posture and muscle tone, and in general had low body energy.

"We never seem to be able to get together on sex," Marcia told me. "We even tried making sexual 'dates' with each other— 'We'll do it tonight,' we promise each other in the morning before we go to work—but then, at night, we get stuck in front of the TV and have a drink or two or three, and then by the time we go to bed one or the other of us is too tired and we make a 'date' for the next night. But then, it's the same story again that night too."

As we talked further, I found there was hardly any anger between these two people—just disappointment and frustration.

"I guess we just can't get used to getting old," Larry said.

"I think you are more than getting used to it," I said. "I think you're making yourselves old before your time."

Before Larry and Marcia could begin to renew their sex life, sexual "foreplay" in the world for them. It was more than just a beginning of a cure: Reviving their energy and recontacting their bodies was all that was standing between Larry and Marcia and the active sex life they had allowed to drift away from them.

Staying in shape physically is a prime way we can stay in shape sexually. By walking, jogging, skiing, playing tennis, or swimming together, we get our hearts beating, our blood flowing, and our "juices" going again. We feel more vital and more sensitive, stronger and less prone to fatigue, and ultimately, we feel more relaxed. Just the smallest regular regimen of exercise can diminish physical tension and emotional stress immeasurably, leaving us both more willing and more able to enjoy ourselves sexually. Recently, volumes have been written about the joys of jogging—physical fitness is enjoying an unprecedented vogue—so I will not go on ad nauseam about the general benefits of getting in shape. But it is worth stressing that sex, first and foremost, is a *physical act:* We simply cannot get sexual until we get physical.

The most satisfying sex begins from a state of complete relaxation, hence the popularity of alcohol as a prelude to sex. But as many have experienced, alcohol or marijuana and most other artificial "relaxants" can be as much an anaphrodisiac—an inhibitor of sex—as a source of arousal. Too much alcohol makes it difficult for many men to achieve a full erection; and for many men and women it promotes so much relaxation that sleep comes more easily than sex. The same can be said of Valium and other popular tranquilizers. As well, many marijuana users have told me that after a while they discovered that smoking before sex can be a game of "Sexual Russian Roulette": Sometimes it heightens sexual sensitivity, but just as often it heightens sexual anxieties.

There is no better way to become relaxed *and* ready for sex than physical exercise. We do not all have to don sweatsuits and jog through the neighborhood—as we have seen, just a *regular,* brisk walk can do wonders. By working out the physical tensions of the day, our sexual energy is easier to release. The fact is, general tensions and anxieties are the major cause of sexual apathy. Specifically, our sexual organs and the muscles surrounding them become more relaxed after a good round of exercise; when these muscles are tight it is more difficult to become aroused. Some couples I know have found that yoga and meditation are a good prelude to sex. "First, I get perfectly relaxed," one yoga practitioner told me, "and then I start concentrating all my energy on my belly and groin and genitals. I think I can literally feel the blood flowing there. And when I'm done, I'm ready to hop into bed."

Marcia added one other reason why exercise turned her on: "It's the sweat. I can't tell you how long it's been since I've sweated from exertion. It just makes me feel so—I don't know— basic, animal. Sweat is sexy."

How our bodies feel to us is one major determinant of how sexual we feel. How we feel *about* our bodies—and each other's —is another.

Age Before Beauty

"I'm too tired for sex" is probably the biggest alibi around for avoiding sex and the anxieties which go with it. But the alibi which comes in a close second is "I'm too old for sex."

This alibi has mythic proportions. On the one hand, it is tied in to The "Real Thing" Myth: Having sex after our reproductive phase of life is over—after we have produced all the children we want or perhaps after menopause—may seem like "illegitimate" sex to us. Yes, we do it now and then, but it would be "inappropriate" to be as active sexually now as when we were making children (as if, in our twenties and thirties we *only* made love to reproduce). A corollary to this idea is that "sex is for the young and beautiful." The media go a long way in promoting this particular myth: On television, in movies, and in popular novels, only women with firm breasts and taut bellies and men with muscular chests and full heads of hair make passionate love. Sure, there are occasional elderly lovers portrayed, but theirs are invariably sentimental affairs, lots of handholding, but not a hint of hot lovemaking. The idea comes across loud and clear: Sex is for the young; it is scandalous for older people to indulge in it.

Both these ideas, of course, are patently absurd, yet it is amazing how subtly they creep into our consciousness. One woman I know told me that her widowed, seventy-year-old mother was remarrying in Florida. "It will be nice for her," the daughter told me; "she misses the companionship of marriage."

"She probably misses the sex too," I added.

The woman looked at me as if I had uttered a crude and cruel joke. "She's seventy," she repeated.

"All the more reason to want regular sex," I said. "Sex is even more comforting then—and she probably has more time for it too."

Anyone who has worked in an old-age home knows that among those healthy enough, "hanky-panky" goes on all the time. The need for and satisfaction from sex does not simply disappear when we grow older and less youthfully attractive; if anything, the need grows. Sex, above all, can keep us in touch with the vibrancy of life.

But it is not people in their seventies and eighties who are most apt to latch onto the "I'm too old for sex" alibi: It is people in their middle age, their forties and fifties. In this period of life, a period which is frequently fraught with career, money, and family anxieties, the "too old for sex" line is a convenient excuse for not dealing with the real causes of sexual apathy.

"It's natural to slow down in your fifties," one man argued with me. "I mean, after all these years, the old 'tank' starts to get empty."

"I hope you don't mean your seminal tank," I told him, "because that keeps replenishing itself daily until the day you die."

And one fifty-year-old woman told me that "as I expected, my sex drive dropped off right after menopause."

"It probably dropped off *because* you expected it to," I told her. "For most women, it can mark the beginning of more relaxed and sensitive sex."

The old adage "we don't get older, just better" is an apt description of our sexual potential. Age really does go before beauty and youth when it comes to lovemaking. In middle age, it is easier for us to let go of our performance and competitive anxieties in bed; these seem like childish preoccupations after years of happy lovemaking. We do not have to prove anything anymore, just enjoy ourselves. For men who have suffered performance anxieties about coming too quickly, age has another advantage: Middle-aged men naturally become less "trigger happy" and their new "staying power" allows both husband and wife more luxuriant lovemaking. Also, despite myths to the contrary, most middle-aged and postmenopausal women are generally more sensitive to touch and more easily aroused than younger women. This is the result of the sexual relaxation which comes from The "Real Thing" Myth in reverse: Without reproduction—and contraception—to worry about, sex can be focused on for its own pleasure. One exception is older women with gynecological problems which make intercourse painful; however, most such problems are easily remedied with proper medical care.

There is another advantage to being middle-aged lovers: familiarity. For a couple who have made love to one another over the course of twenty or thirty years, sexual familiarity can breed contentment instead of contempt. There is a relaxed pleasure which can come from knowing each other's bodies so intimately —each dip and turn and secret spot—and there is a special pleasure in being able to anticipate each other's responses—the particular sensitivity of her nipples or the way he likes to have his testicles cupped or a favorite position when you are both in a particular mood. There are none of the anxieties of guesswork, of wondering if you are "doing it right." As one happily married, middle-aged man described it to me, "Sometimes I think of my wife and myself as two contented barnyard animals who make love together as easily as we eat or sleep together. We're just well mated."

Such sexual contentedness is potentially available to most of us—if we allow it to be. It is the flip side of being numbed by the everydayness of our lives together. We have talked at length about the dangers of falling into unadventurous and boring sexual routines over the years; let us not forget the comforts and relaxed pleasures which can come from routines.

Love Thyself

One "routine" that often causes couples to drift into sexual apathy is making love in the same position every time. Today, there is hardly a couple who do not know most of the alternatives to the "standard" Missionary Position (the woman lying on her back, the man lying on top of her), yet somehow many couples never get around to experimenting with these alternatives, especially the option of the woman on top, sitting astride her husband. As we have seen, some men resist this position because not being in the "dominant" position, not being "in control," makes them anxious. And many women resist this option for a similar reason: It makes them feel "too aggressive" and not "ladylike" enough. But there is another reason why women often resist being on top, even though they may long for some variety of sexual position: *They are embarrassed about how they look.*

On top, a woman's torso—her breasts and belly—are in full view of her partner as compared to the Missionary Position where, face to face, he sees hardly any of her body. And for a woman who is unhappy with the way her torso looks—especially the way her breasts look—the "shame" she feels in being looked at while making love is often enough to keep her from relaxing into her sexual feelings.

"I just can't feel sexy when I'm on display like that," one woman admitted to me. "I keep seeing myself as Bill must see me. . . . how my left breast is lower than my right one, the way they both are beginning to sag, the scar from my caesarean. I'm not exactly a go-go girl up there."

"Has Bill complained about the way you look?" I asked her. "He's said right in this office that he gets turned on by looking at you."

Most of us, women and men alike, have disastrous ideas of how we look. We can go on for hours cataloging what is "wrong" with our bodies—each sag and crease, each blemish and bulge. I do not believe I have met a woman yet who is completely happy with her thighs. Every woman in America seems to think she was singled out by her Maker to have fat or shapeless thighs. Rare, too, is the woman who is completely pleased with how her breasts look: They are too small or too big or asymmetrical; they hang too low; the nipples are not "rosy" enough. The real problem with breasts, it seems, is that they do not look the way they did on our Barbie dolls or the way they look now on starlets and siliconized Playmates—large as melons, hard as rubber balls, and nipples pointing skyward like beacons. Stuck with these bizarre ideals, we are doomed to self-consciousness and shame. How confused we all are about how our breasts *should* look is demonstrated by the statistics on cosmetic breast surgery: In America, the great majority of women who elect such surgery have their breasts enlarged; in the Netherlands, the majority of those who undergo the operation have theirs reduced in size. The "perfect" breast does not seem to exist anywhere else than in our imaginations.

If we are convinced that we "look awful," how can we possibly make un-self-conscious, uninhibited love? With all the lights off and the sheets pulled up to our chins? That seems like a terrible limitation to put on ourselves, one that eliminates taking visual sensual pleasure in one another—pushing us further into depths of sexual dissatisfaction. But making love when we are unhappy about the way we look is like going to a party in a dress we are convinced is ugly: All we can think about is that dress. And worse, *feeling* unattractive, we *become* unattractive to our partners.

"Gail has complained about her thighs for so long that she finally has me convinced they're terrible," one husband told me.

A bad self-image is self-fulfilling. Beautiful you are if you think you are, just as our mothers told us. Men or women who act and carry themselves as if they are attractive, *are* attractive to others. Unfortunately, the opposite is also true, and a bad self-image is what most of us live with.

One requirement I make of every person or couple who come to see me is that they immediately purchase a full-length mirror and install it in their bedroom. It is time to start *really* looking at ourselves—and to start looking good to ourselves. Here is the first "Love Thyself" Exercise which I suggest:

> For five private minutes each day, get undressed and look yourself over—head to toe—in front of a full-length mirror. *Focus on what you find attractive.* This is not just some Pollyanna exercise of seeing the "good" and "beautiful" in everything: All of us have lines and parts and special angles of our bodies which we like, just as when we look at our faces in the mirror we have favorite "views" and "poses" which please us. Don't look at your "figure"; look at pleasing lines and forms. For once, focus on what you like about your body instead of what you do not like.
>
> And all the while, talk to yourself, giving a running commentary on what you see; for example, say, "There is something soft and inviting-looking about my neck, isn't there? No wonder he likes to snuggle there."
>
> or:
>
> "When I turn this way, the line of my breast is rather nice—like a statue."
>
> or (a man):
>
> "When I stand straight, my shoulders do have a strong, square look. Not bad."
>
> Don't miss a spot. Give yourself a real once-over.

The fact is that most people who do not like their bodies rarely, if ever, look at their bodies. Most of their self-images reside solely in their imaginations. Just looking at our bodies five minutes a day can change all of that—and in my experience, usually does. Just the sheer act of looking at our bodies makes us more comfortable with them. We begin to see that our bodies, like our faces, are expressions of who we are. As one woman told me, "I remember one day, while I was doing the exercise, it dawned on me that all those years I'd been feeling awful because I didn't look like Bo Derek. But then I pictured my head —*me*—on Bo Derek's body and the image was just so ludicrous that I started to laugh. And then it occurred to me that if I changed everything—my head too—I wouldn't be me anymore."

Camus once said that every man (and woman) over the age of forty was responsible for the way he looked. He did not mean that if we did not keep a strict diet and do our Jane Fonda exercises every day, we had ourselves to blame; he meant that by the time we reach forty our faces and bodies are expressions of who we are, of how we live and have lived. Liking ourselves and liking our bodies are inseparable ideas. And just as we cannot accept love until we love ourselves, we cannot uninhibitedly and un-self-consciously share our bodies with our partners until we are happy with our bodies ourselves.

The next step of the Love Thyself mirror exercise is more difficult for most of us to try—it is taking a good close look at our genitals.

"Yuk!" I can hear you protesting—the initial reaction of most of the people I give this exercise to. *"If you don't mind, I don't think I want to get to know myself that well. Anyway, aren't some things better left a little mysterious?"*

The so-called "mystery" of our sex organs is that we think they are ugly—droopy, unaesthetic, *raw-* and *dirty*-looking appendages which are better off left hidden from sight. All of this, of course, without ever looking at them—nay, *because* we never look at them.

This shame about our sex organs all began, as the story goes, with Adam and Eve. From an early age, we are taught to keep covered up "down there," to keep our hands away from "down there," and most particularly, we are taught that it is *dirty* "down there." The message lingers with us in peculiar ways; for example, most grown men still wash their hands *after* they urinate—*after* they have handled their penises—rather than before, as if their hands would get dirty from their penises rather than the other way around. Yes, we still believe it is dirty "down there" even though we keep it wrapped and covered all day long.

It is these "unattractive" and "dirty" parts of our bodies which we share with one another in sex. Is it any wonder that we are shy and ashamed when we crawl into bed and that this shame makes us less than free, uninhibited lovers? This exercise is designed to help loosen up these inhibitions:

Standing in front of a mirror, take a good look at your genitals. The first time, do it dispassionately, objectively—a doctor performing an examination.

(Women) With both hands, spread your *labia majora*—the outer lips of your vagina—and peer inside. Put a smaller mirror on the floor and stand above it for a different view, then sit in front of the mirror for a closer view.

(Men) Lift your penis, pull back the foreskin, and take a good look at the head and underside of your penis.

Describe out loud what you see.

Again, just the mere act of objectively looking at our genitals can go a long way in making us more comfortable with them. They do not, after all, look quite so "grotesque" or "dirty" as we may have pictured them in our imaginations. They are simply unfamiliar parts of us, like knees and buttocks—they are not some radically different "thing" which was attached at the last minute to our otherwise pristine bodies.

The Thirty-Year Blind Date

A few years ago, a couple in their mid-fifties came to see me because they had not made love at all in a year and the husband, especially, was terribly disturbed and frustrated by the absence of sex in his life. In the course of finding out more about the two of them, I asked them each to describe a typical evening of lovemaking before it came to an end.

"It was perfectly normal," the wife told me. "I usually got into bed first and turned off the light and waited for Bob to get in beside me. Then we'd embrace and kiss and after a while, I'd pull off my nightgown and Bob would slip off his pajamas and we'd begin. . . ."

What was "perfectly normal" for this couple, it turned out, was to make love without ever seeing each other's nude bodies. In fact, they had been on a thirty-year blind date. Little wonder that after all those years, they were still not genuinely comfortable with each other in bed. Each other's bodies remained alien, shameful things. They had taken modesty to such an extreme that it had eventually eliminated sex altogether.

This couple were clearly an old-fashioned extreme, yet to a lesser degree many of us remain somewhat uncomfortable with one another's bodies. We never really take a good, languorous look at one another anymore. And, for many of us, there are parts of our partner's bodies that we perpetually close our eyes to.

One woman I know who had an active sex life with her husband admitted to me that she never looks at her husband's penis when she touches it. "I just automatically look somewhere else or close my eyes," she said. "What can I tell you? It looks like an angry, red cyclops to me."

This woman had an active, frequent sex life, yet she was seeing me because sex was rarely completely satisfying for her. But how could sex be satisfying when she found her husband's penis—penises in general, for that matter—so unattractive she could not look at it? How could she begin to feel comfortable with sex if she was not comfortable with the most sexual part of her husband's body?

I have also spoken to many men who have an automatic aversion to looking at parts of their wives' bodies—especially the genital parts. To really look at their wives' vaginas makes them extremely anxious and, in some cases, turns them right off. The simple fact is that we cannot have truly satisfying sex if we are not comfortable with each other's bodies—visually as well as tactilely.

There are many ways we can *be nude together* which can make us less anxious and more comfortable with each other's bodies. And these do not have to be potentially sexual situations in the sense that they are the prelude to sexual contact; but at the very least they are situations where sex is a *possibility,* where sexual contact might—but does not have to—happen.

To the couple who had been on the thirty-year blind date, I suggested the following exercise:

Take turns washing each other's hair. To begin, if it makes you more comfortable, wear bathing suits in the bathroom. Make it a real head massage. And while you are doing it, look at your partner's body carefully. Focus on what you find attractive about it. If you feel like it, tell your partner what you are thinking.

Later, after you are more comfortable with each other, do the same exercise without bathing suits.

This is the sort of thing many of us used to do spontaneously early in our relationship—why did we ever stop? Washing each other's hair, massaging each other with oils and lotions, giving each other haircuts—these are the simple activities which can bring us closer to one another in ways which long talks and going out to dinner and the movies never can. Nude together in a relaxed atmosphere—without any sexual demand and the anxieties which may come with it—we can look at one another with pleasure. By simply touching and massaging each other, we start to feel relaxed and comfortable with one another. We feel good, so we feel good about each other. And frequently sexual contact follows naturally.

Sex rarely begins at the height of passion. It begins with a relaxed appreciation of one another's bodies.

The Case Against Twin Beds

When I first learned English, I was amazed to discover that the expression "sleeping together" meant the same thing as "having sex together." "Sleeping is sleeping and sex is sex," I thought, "and who can make love in his sleep?"

I was wrong. As it turns out, we all make love in our sleep in a sense. Sleep is a sexual activity—over the course of a night's sleep we all become aroused and rearoused several times. Sleep, then, is a natural segue to sex: In the middle of the night or early in the morning we can slide very naturally from dreamy arousal to sexual contact with our partner. What a shame that in practice so many of us keep "sleeping together" and "having sex together" as separate activities.

My personal opinion is that the adoption of separate twin beds in marriage has done more to diminish marital sex than anyone suspects. Going to sleep without touching at all—no arm flung across a chest, no cheek snuggled against a neck—we have abandoned the best natural "foreplay" in the world. As well, sleeping together in the nude seems to be a lost art these days and a great potential of sexuality has been lost with it. Sleeping apart, our bodies can become alienated from each other. We lose both the comfort and stimulation of casually touching and casually being touched. To couples who come to me complaining of infrequent sex, I often offer this simple advice:

> Turn up the thermostat, leave your pajamas and nightgown in the bureau, and *sleep* together. That's right—just sleep. But fall asleep with your nude bodies touching somehow—in a way which is comfortable for both of you.
> If you both agree, make this deal with one another: that either of you can wake the other up at any time to make love.

Most couples are amazed by how this simple change in pattern can revitalize their sex lives without any apparent effort.

"Hold on!" I can hear some of you protesting. *"The whole reason why we got separate beds in the first place was so we could have a decent, uninterrupted night of sleep. And neither of us can really sleep with an arm or leg flung over us."*

I am well aware that many couples opt for separate beds because one or both partners cannot comfortably fall asleep in contact with the other's body. One complains that the other "jumps around" too much. The other complains that she feels like she is "being crushed." Both complain about "space wars" —nudging the other to the edge of the bed—and "blanket wars"—an all-night tug-of-war. And I suppose in some of these cases separate beds is the best, most "peaceful" solution. But again, so much sexual potential is lost this way that I think it is worth a try to *relearn* how to sleep together in physical contact. Just a foot touching a foot can make all the difference. And when we give this idea a chance we very soon may discover that physical contact which once felt "irritating" or "oppressive" now begins to feel like a source of relaxed pleasure—especially if we find that we are making love more often.

"I'll Show You Mine, If You'll Show Me Yours"

There is probably no better way for becoming comfortable with each other's sex organs than by playing a game of "I'll Show You Mine, If You'll Show Me Yours"—but this time, it is not a forbidden game. Before anyone can protest that this is "too childish" for them, let me say once again that the very best sex we can have is playful and childish, even regressive. There is nothing "mature" about sex in itself—only in its consequences and implications. Playing "I'll Show You Mine . . ." can put us in a relaxed, even giddy mood that goes a long way toward reducing whatever anxieties we may have about looking closely at one another's bodies.

Begin, both nude, in front of the full-length, bedroom mirror. One at a time, look at yourself in the same way you have looked at yourself alone before. Go from head to toe, focusing on what you like about your body. Don't miss anything. Tell your partner what you see and what you like.

Now, focus on your genitals using the smaller mirror if you like. Using your hands, show your partner your genitals—the "ins and outs," the specially sensitive spots.

Next, bring the "game" to bed and play "Doctor" with each other.

Taking turns, give each other's genitals a thorough "examination." See what they are all about, how they work, always touching them gently.

This is not a "sexual" game *per se;* it does not necessarily lead to arousal or sexual contact. It is simply a way to become desensitized to any anxieties you may have about each other's genitals —about looking at them, or having someone look at yours. For some couples who are particularly disturbed—consciously or unconsciously—by the "dirtiness" of sexual organs, I suggest that they take the game to the bathroom and wash each other's genitalia while inspecting them.

But this "innocent" game need not end here. Many couples I know have found a great deal of relaxed, amusing—even hilarious—pleasure in playing like children with each other's sex organs. One woman told me that she got "carried away" and started tying ribbons around her husband's penis; another told me that she started singing to her husband's penis— "It looked like a microphone to me," she laughed. And one man told me that he brought a flashlight to bed when they played "Doctor." All told me that they had thoroughly enjoyed themselves.

"What a relief it was just to play," one of them said.

"You Can't Turn It Down Until You've Tasted It"

As in many homes, my parents had a simple rule about food: "You don't have to eat everything. But you can't turn anything down until you've tasted it."

It is a reasonable rule and I find that it applies fittingly to sex too. When it comes to sexual secretions—semen or vaginal secretions—I say don't turn them down until you have tasted them.

Many of us feel that these natural secretions are "dirty," the very idea of putting them in our mouths makes us terribly uncomfortable. And hence we miss out on a very enjoyable sexual variation, one that could make married sex an adventure again—oral-genital stimulation. If we have an aversion to taking sexual secretions into our mouths, what does that tell us about how we feel about our sex organs? A woman who tells me that it is fine if her husband ejaculates into her vagina but she does not want that "awful stuff" in her mouth is saying, in effect, that her vagina is a garbage can. It is okay for that "awful stuff" to be deposited there.

"Don't be absurd!" (That voice of protest again.) *"There is a big difference between my vagina and my mouth. For one thing I don't have to Taste semen in my vagina."*

True. And that is just my point. Let us once and for all taste each other's secretions and decide if we really want to "turn them down." This applies to *both* partners—for *both* of your secretions. Too many times I have heard men complain that they feel "rejected" by their wives because they refuse to let them come in their mouths or because they refuse to swallow their semen—yet these same men feel queasy about kissing their wives if their wives' lips have their semen on them. Likewise, there are many women who long to have their husbands perform oral sex on them, but the very idea of kissing afterward makes them uncomfortable. Somewhere along the line we have associated our sexual secretions with excrement—our bodies' wastes, rather than with our bodies' "love juices." We do not have an aversion to tasting each other's tears, why should we have one to tasting our sexual secretions? As I say, let us not turn them down until we have tasted them at least once:

> Take turns dipping your fingers into a pool of his semen as if you were sampling a new "sauce." Describe what you taste to one another.

> Next, take turns "sampling" her vaginal secretions—another "sauce." Again, describe the taste to one another.

The results of this exercise for most people range from "it wasn't so bad" to "yummy"; rarely is it as distasteful as we expected. As one woman reported jokingly telling her husband after sampling his semen, "If you added a little pepper and basil, you might have something there."

The idea of this, as of all the exercises in this chapter, is simply to remove the anxieties and aversions which stand in the way of our bodies "making friends" with each other. Because "friendly" bodies make better love together.

11
The Art of Using
Each Other

An attractive couple in their mid-thirties, Penny and Rick L., beset by what they called "the sexual doldrums," came to me in hopes of discovering what had gone wrong in their marriage. For the first few years before and after they had married, sex had been marvelous for both of them; but then, as Penny put it, "It started to become a chore and then a bore."

"What did you use to do together that you don't do anymore?" I asked them.

Both Penny and Rick shrugged. "We still do everything more or less the same," Rick said. "But we don't seem to be able to get into it the way we used to."

"Maybe it's time to do something different with each other," I said. "Your sexual tastes change, you know, just like your tastes for food and books and everything else. Have you talked to each other recently about your fondest sexual desires? About what you'd like your partner to do to you in bed—where you want to be touched and how?"

Again, they both shrugged and looked somewhat embarrassed. After a little coaxing, Penny told me what put her off about talking with Rick about what she wanted from him in bed: "It seems to me that spelling things out like that takes all the magic out of sex. It seems so darned matter-of-fact to sit there and say, 'I want you to touch me here like this and there like that.' No romance, just taking care of business. Before, I never had to do that. Rick always knew exactly what I wanted without my having to tell him."

"And if he can't read your mind now," I said ironically, "then you aren't going to tell him, right? I mean, if he really loved you, he'd know exactly what you want without having to ask."

Penny gave me a reluctant smile. "Well, something like that," she said.

Too many couples get stuck with The "If You Really Loved Me You'd Know Exactly What I Want" Myth and end up going to bed night after night never really getting what they want at all. They say that a Perfect Lover would know "instinctively" what would turn them on just by looking in their eyes and at their bodies, just by touching them. And they say that something must be missing in their relationship if their lover does not have (or has lost) this "instinct."

Soulmates provide another self-defeating variation on this myth: "We are so much the same," they say, "that I just assume that what feels good to me must feel good to my partner too—so there's no need to break the magic by talking about it." These are people who would feel that they were not "close enough" if it turned out that their real sexual tastes were somewhat different from each other's, that one would rather be touched here and the other there. Penny and Rick were holding tight to yet another variation of The "If You Really Loved Me" Myth—"The Myth of the Unchangeable Partner." They told me that they were still doing the same things in bed that they had when they first got married and Penny insisted that in those "good old days" Rick did not have to ask what pleased her. Somehow, it had never occurred to either of them that the other's sexual tastes had changed, that, say, Penny had discovered a more sensitive spot where she wanted to be touched, or that Rick had been playing a new sexual fantasy in his mind for months which he wanted to try. But more to the point, it had not occurred to either of them to *express* these changes to each other—all in the name of "Love." The most startling example of The Unchangeable Partner Myth I ever encountered occurred in my office when a woman said that she longed for her husband to caress her breasts.

"But you told me you don't like your breasts touched," her husband protested.

"That was fifteen years ago," his wife replied.

Taken together, these variations on The "If You Really Loved Me You'd Know Exactly What I Want" Myth constitute one of the most destructive of the "romantic" myths and, it seems to me, one of the most absurd ones. Would we ever expect our partner to order for us in a restaurant—to know "instinctively" that we'd rather have sole than salmon, or blue cheese dressing than Italian tonight? I think not. Then why do we carry the same impossible idea into the bedroom?

The answer lies not so much in "romance" as in embarrassment. We are afraid to come out and say what we really want from each other in bed because we do not want to appear *selfish* —to our partners or to ourselves. That is the worst of sexual "sins": It means, without alibis or excuses, that we really want to enjoy as much sexual pleasure as possible.

The First Commandment of Married Sex: Please Thyself

"Selfishness" has gotten a bad name in sex, especially married sex. The very idea of being self-centered in the marriage bed— of just *focusing on* and *asking for* what feels good *to you*—is enough to make most people cringe with embarrassment.

"But what makes a marriage work is giving and sharing," people protest when I suggest they try being more sexually selfish with one another. "We have to compromise to keep each other satisfied. Marriage is a 50-50 proposition."

Or they say:

"True love is selfless. It means not asking for anything—especially in bed."

Or they say:

"Selfish sex is for pigs and nymphomaniacs. I only want caring sex, thank you."

But to all of these protests I reply, "Selfish sex is the very best way for *both of you* to enjoy each other. Two selfish people in bed *both* get what they want. Instead of a 50-50 proposition, married sex should be a 100-100 proposition. And if that means you are both sexual pigs, fine, because sensual 'pigs' have a lot more fun in bed than people who are so concerned with sacrifice and compromise and pleasing each other that they never feel absolutely satisfied themselves."

Earlier, we saw how the Don Juans and other sexual performers of the world who are preoccupied with pleasing their partners and flattering themselves often miss out on sexual pleasure because they do not concern themselves enough with their own sexual feelings—in short, egoistic as they may seem, ultimately they are not selfish enough. Likewise, the Hard Workers and Dutiful Wives who make a career of "doing it right" and "giving in" ultimately make lovemaking a joyless enterprise by focusing all their attentions on their partners' responses and none on their own. As well, the "feminine" women who insist that it would be "unladylike" to be aggressive in bed and the "macho" men who insist that it would be humiliating to be passive in bed all sacrifice sexual satisfaction because they are afraid of being "pigs."

But the fact is that sex which is always aimed at pleasing your partner or achieving some "masculine" or "feminine" ideal often leads to sexual boredom and frustration. And all it takes is one sexually dissatisfied partner to eventually kill a relationship. In the long run it is not sexual *selfishness* which takes its toll on a marriage—it is sexual *selflessness*.

Learning How to Be a Pig

"My husband never just comes out and asks me for sex," one woman told me. "Instead, he wanders around the house in a blue funk for a couple of days until I ask him what's wrong and then he grumbles, 'What's wrong? We haven't had sex in a week, that's what's wrong!'"

And one man told me that his wife never says to him that she wants to have sex, "She waits until I initiate it and then, just when I'm getting started, she says, 'I've been hinting at this all week— I wondered when you'd finally get the idea.' "

In both cases, the partners could not simply say what they wanted and the result, when sex finally did "happen" was joyless, begrudging lovemaking—all because they were too shy or embarrassed to be "selfish."

"Learning How to Be a Pig" requires that we stop seeing sexual "selfishness" in a negative way and start seeing it as taking joy in a positive way. "Using each other" *is* positive; it is an act of trust and affection, just as "using" your favorite shirt or tennis racket or restaurant is a clear sign of the affection you feel for the familiar objects in your life. *Sexual selfishness means satisfying yourself completely with the help of your partner.* It means changing marriage-long patterns of *how* you get sexual satisfaction and *who* initiates sex: Instead of getting depressed, claiming that you're sick, or bullying your partner to get him or her to have sex with you, it means overcoming your shyness and embarrassment and all your other reluctances and *directly asking your partner for sex.*

Instead of waiting in frustration and anger for your partner to "read your mind" about your sexual desires and needs, it means *showing your partner what you like and exactly how you like it.*

Instead of playing "Martyr" or "Lady," "Mr. Polite" or "Super Lover," it means *focusing on and going for your own sexual pleasure—First!*

"Hold it right there," I can hear some of you protesting. *"You make it sound like only one partner is going to end up satisfied —the selfish one."*

No, not the selfish *one*—the selfish *two:* Both of you. The last thing I am suggesting is that one partner be the "sacrificer" or the "compromiser"; rather I am suggesting that both partners make a deal to *satisfy each other* and to do it *exactly the way your partner wants.* There is a world of difference between one partner being selfless and both partners being "mutually generous."

This "deal" is a serious one and it is a hard one for many people to make, but if it is tried in the spirit of a game or exercise, the whole focus of your sex life can begin to change:

Give and Ye Shall Receive

Make a deal with one another for the next two weeks to ask for whatever you want sexually when you want it!

Do not wait until you think your partner is receptive or in the "right mood." Do not give in to your "natural" inclination to be shy or embarrassed. And do not be afraid to *very explicitly show* or *say* exactly what you desire.

Give permission to each other to ask for anything at all, even to wake you up at three in the morning and say, "Now."

But always allow your partner to reserve the prerogative to say, "I'm not in the mood for a big production right now, but if you want, I'd be happy to masturbate you . . . or simply to hold you while you masturbate." And accept these answers without an argument.

Ask for your *wildest desires.* Do not censor yourself by think-ing that your desire is too "wild" or "crazy" or "dirty." And do not try to second-guess whether or not your partner would really like to try it. Go ahead and ask, you may be surprised by your partner's response—it might turn out to be his or her "wildest desire" too. There is no harm in asking and there need not be any harm or hurt in being refused all that you want.

And don't worry if your "wildest desire" is rather tame or even if you don't have any "crazy" fantasies. You are not out to break any records, just to satisfy yourself—*exactly the way you want.*

If either of you feels the "deal" may turn out to be unequal, specify *how many* "sexual favors" each of you can ask for over those two weeks.

Finally, and most importantly, *focus on your own* sexual feel-ings and sensations, not on your partner's. In fact, to begin, forget about your partner. Close your eyes if it makes it easier to concentrate on just what you are feeling. And if you start to feel guilty about your "selfishness" chase it from your mind by remembering that your partner's turn is next: That is what mutual generosity is all about.

Like the touching exercises in Part I, the success of this exercise is dependent on your *taking turns;* but unlike the touching exercises, this one is no holds barred. The idea is to free us up to ask for *anything.*

"But what if my partner is revolted by my 'wildest desire?'" I can hear you fretting.

That can happen. In fact, it often does, and, for the moment, you can end up feeling quite embarrassed. Here you have summoned up all your courage to reveal your most secret of secrets and your partner responds by saying disdainfully, "You want *that?"* Most likely, you will wish you had never opened your mouth: You were feeling guilty about your fantasy in the first place and now you feel downright "perverse."

But take a moment before you give up on the whole adventure of sharing your fantasies. Here, more than ever, patience and understanding can pay off in the long run. Remember first that male and female sexual fantasies are often quite different: What seems "perverse" to her may seem quite "normal" to him and vica versa. It also helps to recall how "yukky" *all of sex* seemed to us as children: When a child first hears what sexual intercourse is all about it sounds positively disgusting to him. It may take time for your partner to accept your wildest desire, to grow into the idea. One "yuk" need not close the door forever to expanding our sexual repertoire to include our every desire.

Only in a committed relationship can we dare to take our fantasies all the way. In casual sex, free as it may seem, we are always aware of the risk of permanently putting our partner off by voicing our wildest desires. But in a long-term "deal," knowing that "tomorrow is *your* turn," we can dare to be "selfish"— to try again another day.

Man Enough to Be Passive/Woman Enough to Be Active

Probably the chief way that men end up missing out on the joys of "selfish" sex is by feeling "honor bound" always to be the aggressor, the one who initiates sex, and who controls the course of lovemaking. It is primary to the popular idea of masculinity, and it is an idea which many women hold as well. Yet most men's sexual fantasies often feature scenes of them lying back while a woman ministers to their every sexual desire, doing all the "work" while they relax in pure pleasure. Some men play out this secret fantasy in "massage parlors" with prostitutes, but at home they fall right back into their aggressor role and miss out on a lot of the fun. Most men see an aggressive wife as a threat, a demand for them to perform, or worse they see an active wife as infantilizing—forcing them to be an "obedient child." We have already explored some ways for men to disengage themselves from the thankless role of "constant aggressor" —touching exercises are one step toward this goal, the UnMom-mying exercises are another—but an even more positive step in this direction is to focus on our passive fantasies. It is the first step in making them come true:

Let Her Do the Work

Imagine you are in a massage parlor. You have paid your money and now you lie naked on the "massage" table. A naked woman enters and tells you that she will do anything to you that you want—your every sexual wish is her command. She says, "Just lie there" while she does all the "work."

When it is your turn to be "selfish" with your partner—part of your deal—make your fantasy come true. Make your bedroom the "massage parlor" and let your partner do all the "work."

If you begin to feel anxious or inadequate because you are not in control, push the anxiety away by concentrating on the fantasy and your feelings. Remember, you have "paid" for this privilege in the deal you made with your partner.

And do not worry that you will become "addicted" to passive sex—it is just one more way you can add variety to your sex life.

Most men who try this exercise admit that they have experienced sensations which have eluded them most of their adult lives. For the first time since they were babies they can passively have their sensual desires answered. And as for their fear of being infantilized or emasculated by this passive experience, they very quickly learn that they do not *remain a baby* after the experience is over. As soon as they stand up, they are "grown up" again. In fact, most men make the paradoxical discovery that only by allowing themselves such "regressions" can they really be mature, only by "relaxing like a baby" once in a while can they lead forceful and stress-free adult lives, both in and out of bed. As one man told me, "It's hard to imagine that I've been married for fifteen years and I never even thought of asking my wife to just 'do me' for once. I don't think I've ever relaxed during sex so much before."

Nor had he ever been that "selfish" before.

Women frequently deny themselves sexual pleasure in a similar way: Afraid that it would be "unladylike" to be aggressive, they spend their lives lying passively and holding back their active impulses. As we have seen, for many of these women the real fear is that they will lose their "passive control"—their power to use their sexual favors, their yesses and nos, to keep their partners dependent on them. Again, the best route out of this self-denying trap is to get in touch with our fantasies. Again and again women tell me that one of their wildest desires is to have a "slave" lover, a man they can *use* to satisfy their every sexual whim. It is a fantasy which can be part of any couple's deal.

"Slave" for the Night

Imagine you have a lover who will do whatever you ask of him, who will obey your every command. Fantasize about how you would *use his body* to fulfill your sexual desires.

When it is your turn to be "selfish" with your partner, make this fantasy come true. Make your partner your "slave" for the night—make his body your "lollipop." If you begin to feel anxious because you feel you are being "unladylike," push the anxiety away by concentrating on your fantasy and feelings. Remember, it is the privilege allowed you by the deal you made with your partner. His turn is coming.

In both of these exercises, one partner is in the position of *demanding* sexual satisfaction from the other, but the exercises will be easier for both of you if the demands are posed in a positive way. Instead of sexual nagging which can bring all sex to a standstill—the negative "You-never-give-me-enough-of-this-or-that"—say, "What I'd really love now is this-or-that." It makes it a lot easier for your partner to give a positive response. But we cannot forget that your partner always reserves the prerogative to say, "I'm not ready for this fantasy yet, but I'm willing to do something else in the meantime." And again, this must be seen in a positive light. The "No" is a "No-for-now," not an outright sexual rejection forever. It would be against the spirit of the deal to let one "No" prevent you from asking for a particular fantasy again—even the next night.

How to Be "Generous" Without Making It a "Sacrifice"

"Giving in" to your partner's sexual demands is a drag; it virtually guarantees that you will not feel very much as you grudgingly "go through the motions." But when you know that you do not have to give any more than you want to—that it is perfectly fair to say, for example, "I'm not up for much tonight, but I'll be glad to masturbate you" or, "I'm kind of tired, let's just do it the 'lazy way' [see Chapter 14, "Sexual Smorgasbord"] and call it a night"—then sex immediately becomes less of a threatening "big production" and more of a casual-but-caring part of your daily life. It puts it all on the same level as saying *(generously)*, "I'm not hungry tonight, but I'll be glad to make you a sandwich" instead of saying *(martyrishly)*, "Okay, I'll give in tonight, but remember, this is just for you."

This switch in attitude can make all the difference in our sex lives. Instead of one partner martyred and the other guilty, we end up with two guiltlessly happy and sexually content people. By making the deal to "do each other," sexual duty very quickly transforms itself into sexual pleasure. Like parents who hug their children out of love rather than out of duty, we rediscover the sensual satisfaction of "giving" as compared to "giving in." Ironically, *selfish sex*—giving only what you want to give— turns out to be the most *generous sex* there is.

12
Take Each Other— and a Sandwich—to Bed

"We're Too Busy for Sex"

That is the most common complaint I hear, especially today with both husbands and wives working. But invariably my response is, "Nonsense!"

I've talked to hundreds of couples "too busy for sex" who think nothing of dedicating a full hour to the preparation of their dinners, who somehow manage to spend at least an hour watching television each evening, and who average two nights out a week with friends, at classes, gyms, or meetings. In terms of everyday priorities, sex comes in last, far behind Chicken Sienna, Dan Rather, and exercising their bodies to perfection. They have literally scheduled sex right out of their lives.

For most of us, being "too busy" is simply another subtle way we avoid sex—another way we turn ourselves off without honestly confronting what we are doing. We say, "Look at all the virtuous things I *am* doing—the PTA committee meetings, the aerobic dancing, the classes, the concerts" and so we never have to think about what we are *not* doing and why. By not having time for sex, we never have to face the anxieties or resentments which are the real reasons why we haven't made love for weeks or months on end.

One woman was on the verge of tears when she said to me, "Every night when I go to bed and see his back lying there next to me, all I can think is: Here's one more day that we won't make love. It's six weeks now."

Yet as I talked further with this woman, I found that she went to aerobic exercise classes three nights a week while her husband stayed home alone. It was not long before she was able to admit to herself that she was ashamed of some weight she had put on and that she wasn't going to allow herself to feel sexual until she thought she looked good again.

And one couple I saw had fallen into a terrible depression because they had made love only once in three months, but again, when we examined their schedules, we found that they had barely left themselves a moment for relaxed lovemaking. It turned out that each of them was using busyness to bury old resentments: She resented the fact that for years they made love only when he wanted to; and he resented that she was losing sexual interest in him. Instead of facing their resentments, they had stopped facing each other in bed.

For most of us, the unacknowledged reasons why we leave ourselves so little time for sex are not quite so easy to pinpoint; it is more often a combination of the turnoffs we explored in Part I of this book. But one wonderful thing about sex is that you don't always have to analyze it—you can simply do it and problems seem to solve themselves. The best way I've found for breaking the "too busy" pattern is in one fell swoop—straight into bed. It's an idea so simple that it seems laughable:

One evening a week—Wednesday is a nice, neutral day—pick up a bottle of wine and two sandwiches-to-go on the way home from work, and take each other—and the sandwiches— directly to bed. Do not turn on the TV. Do turn off the phone (or put on your answering machine). And for the next three or four hours, just eat, drink, and *fool around.*

It is usually about here that I am interrupted by laughter, laughter with a slightly nervous ring to it.

"Are you actually suggesting that we schedule our sex?"

Indeed I am. And what is so bizarre about that? Most of us have been scheduling our sex ever since our sex lives began. When we went out on dates, didn't we already know at the beginning of the evening what we were going to do after the movie and in whose apartment we were going to do it? And now, living together, we have undoubtedly developed routines of making love at the same times on the same days—Sunday mornings seem to be the national favorite. So for starters, all I am suggesting is that we make this scheduling conscious and open, that a couple consult each other the same way they would about any other evening appointment and then explicitly set aside time on the calendar for a regular evening of mutual sensual pleasure. In short, that we make sex as important and definite a part of our lives as seeing our friends or watching "The Bill Cosby Show." And don't worry, this scheme doesn't put a limit on unscheduled sexual events; in fact, one magical offshoot of calendar sex is that it usually revitalizes impromptu sex—like the long-forgotten morning "quickie" on the bathroom floor. Regular sex simply gets the old juices flowing again.

"I Really Should Be Doing Something More Important"

For most people who try it, putting a red circle around every Wednesday of the month is a marvelous aphrodisiac in itself. It provides something to fantasize about, something to look forward to.

"I usually start 'cooking' around ten o'clock Wednesday mornings," one woman told me. "I think, 'Wow, what are we going to do tonight?' By three in the afternoon, I've already made one or two 'obscene' phone calls to my husband at his office."

But for others—particularly performance-oriented men—anticipating a whole evening of sex can generate anxiety, at least the first few Wednesdays. By three in the afternoon, *he* is thinking, "Good grief, tonight's the night! What if things don't go right? How will I ever get through it?" As we will see later, the open-ended program for these sensual soirees is set up to defuse anxieties just like these.

The nervous laughter persists.

"Okay, we can schedule weekly sex—but for a whole evening?"

Yes, the whole evening. From the minute you get home until you turn down the thermostat and go to sleep. Three or four hours—the equivalent of dinner and a movie. But this is *not* a sexual marathon we're planning: It's an evening of love play, of sensual games, of reacquainting ourselves with each other's bodies and the gentle pleasures they can afford us. Sexual intercourse will account for just a fraction of the evening (if any of it) —the rest is just a picnic, a very sexy picnic.

Still, the idea of an entire evening devoted to sensual fun and games does not quite sit right with many of us.

"But we truly are busy," one woman protested. "I just don't honestly see how we can fit in a whole evening once a week."

"Four hours seems a little excessive to me," a man told me. "That's an awful lot of unproductive, self-indulgent time."

To all of these protests I can only answer with a question of my own: *"Just how important is sex to you and to your relationship?"*

That question has to be answered honestly and openly before you can go on. Are both of you truly satisfied with the frequency and duration of your "spontaneous" sex lives? Is your sexual relationship really less important than all the other activities which keep you busy and out of bed? Yes, giving yourself and each other pleasure for three or four hours is totally self-indulgent. But is it really any more so than a dinner and movie (which, incidentally, is much more extravagant than a bottle of Chablis and two tuna specials to go)? I think not. And I think any couple who are concerned with keeping their sex lives vital and exciting are ready to give up that "I Really Should Be Doing Something More Important" way of thinking. One or two Wednesday-night picnics are usually enough to convince most couples that this is one self-indulgence they deserve.

A Lot of Time, Nothing to Do

Most couples ask me, "What can you actually do for all that time?"

A great many things—enough for a whole lifetime of Wednesdays, in fact. But to begin with I suggest you uncork the wine and then unwrap your sandwiches and yourselves—any order will do. This is going to be a nude picnic.

(For those who are concerned about crumbs and mayonnaise stains, I recommend spreading a tablecloth over the sheets, or better yet, reserving a special set of linen for Wednesday nights. Also for comfort's sake, I think a variable room heater is a good idea. All practical concerns should be out of the way and out of mind before the evening begins.)

Okay, let's begin. And remember, there is only one rule: *Don't hurry anything.* Many couples I know can spend a good hour just eating and drinking and *looking at each other.* For most of us, it is rare that we leisurely survey each other's nudity. The rest of the week we just glimpse flashes and patches of each other's bodies stepping out of showers and into pajamas. And usually when we make love, we go from undressing to embracing without so much as one long, arm's-length gander at one another in between. Wednesday nights are marvelous nights for long, leisurely ganders.

And talking. Nothing special, just the usual coming-home chatter about what happened at work and the story you read in the *Times.* But you are lying on the bed together and you don't have any clothes on and all the while that you are talking you are looking too. And when you reach out to wipe away that little fleck of mustard on his chin, you linger a moment, tracing the shape of his smile with your fingertips. It is a pleasure, pure and simple and unhurried.

Now there is just a chance that after a while one or both of you will want to touch each other more intimately, but again I say, do yourself a favor—don't hurry. And don't think about what all this is leading up to. Because maybe all this is just leading up to more fondling and talking, eating and looking. And maybe it is all leading up to a sexual surprise that neither of you had planned. One of the wonderful ironies of these scheduled evenings is that they usually include more spontaneous sexual experimentation than an unscheduled evening does. Those unscheduled evenings, it seems, too frequently fall victim to old habits and comfortable—yet uninspiring—routines. Taking your time and maintaining an "anything can happen" attitude can open up a surprise package of sexual delights.

To get things rolling—especially those first few self-conscious Wednesday evenings—you might want to begin by reviewing Touching Exercise #1. This is self-indulgence at its very best:

> With the light on, spread out on your bed while your partner touches and fondles your body everywhere except your genitals (and breasts). Let this go on for at least fifteen minutes, but no more than an hour, and as it is happening express out loud *exactly* what you want—for example, "More slowly, please" or "That feels wonderful when you just skim your fingertips around my belly." Afterward, return the favor.

This simple interlude can set a loving, sensual tone for the rest of the evening. First and foremost, it allows both of you to overcome any shyness you may feel about *asking for pleasure.* You give each other permission to be totally selfish. And by asking, you take away the burden of having to read each other's minds about what feels good. Prolonged sensual touching with no genital contact removes sexual anxieties. In turn, each of you becomes relaxed, sensitized, and responsive. It revives that sense of trust and well-being that many of us have not experienced since we were stroked as children. The end result is that you both emerge from the interlude feeling wonderful about one another. Without argument or analysis, your resentments and recriminations simply evaporate. Making sensual, uninhibited love often follows naturally.

But just maybe—especially that first Wednesday—nothing much will follow at all. Fine. Just keep on eating and talking and looking. Maybe read out loud a little or listen to some music. That first Wednesday may make you feel too giddy and self-conscious to do anything more than that. By keeping the evening open-ended the pressure is taken off both of you. There are no disappointments—silent or otherwise—to worry about. No performances to put in. No orgasms to tally. For the performance-oriented man especially, this *que sera, sera* attitude can mean the difference between anticipating an evening of anxiety or an evening of free and casual pleasure. Many couples I've talked to maintain this casual ambience by mixing things up, doing two or three things at once:

> Sometimes he sprawls on his stomach reading a story from the paper out loud while I sit on his buttocks and rub his back.
> and,
> Once we had the wildest time doing this whole *Tom Jones* number—eating our food as if it were some great erotic act. Half the time we were giggling and the other half we were touching each other all over the place.

By mixing things up, we can break down rigid categorical sequences, break out of the old "first we eat, then we get undressed, then we have foreplay, then we make love, Good night, dear" routine. We can eat and stroke *at the same time.* And we can interrupt intercourse to tell a joke if we want to. No rules, no prescribed sequences. And there is no countdown to the "Main Event" to keep us jittery as prizefighters.

"Isn't It UnRomantic?"

Still, there are many couples who view the "picnic" as "too casual." As one woman said, "Eating tuna fish with one hand and caressing with the other. It sounds terribly unromantic to me."

Not unromantic—just not deadly serious. In short, more fun. When it comes to sex, too many of us become as earnest as little Scouts working on a merit badge. By mixing things up, we can lighten things up. One enthusiastic convert to Wednesday-night picnics put it this way:

What a relief it is to have all that *reverence for sex* out of the way. Of course, the crazy paradox is that now that we treat sex as just another thing we do along with eating sandwiches and doing the crossword puzzle, it's become infinitely more exciting.

And while we're on the subject of what is Romantic Sex—and what isn't—it seems to me that we've trapped ourselves into tired old categories here too. Why should "Romantic Sex" imply only soft lights and champagne, Ravel on the phonograph, and whispered sweet nothings?

Is tuna and the *Times* necessarily any less romantic? Or a pillow fight? Or an under-the-blankets yodeling contest? There's got to be more to romantic sex than what they tell us in perfume ads—in fact the only limits are our own imaginations.

I know one couple who can spend hours finger painting on each other's bodies. Not romantic? That's not what they tell me.

Another couple—she's a stockbroker and he's a lawyer, the most conservative-looking pair I know—tell me that they like to do a little nude tumbling while they listen to circus music. Sounds like fun to me.

Later, in "Sexual Smorgasbord," I'll get into more such games in detail, but for now the point is this: Holding out for some limited idea of "Romantic Sex" is a sure way to miss out on a banquet of sexual fun.

"Look, isn't all this taking-the-pressure-off stuff just an elaborate way of kidding ourselves?" I can hear you grumbling. *"The whole idea of the 'picnic' is that eventually we're going to get down to some real sex, isn't it?"*

Only if that is what both of you want. Honestly. Certainly for most couples, the evening usually includes orgasmic sex along the way. But there will be times when, because of fatigue, anxiety, or simply because you just don't feel like it tonight, orgasmic sex will be skipped this Wednesday, thank you. But that is certainly *no reason* for skipping the whole picnic. You can still take your sandwiches to bed and have a languorous, physically comforting evening together without any genital stimulation at all. Or you can arouse one another, then go on to something else, and arouse one another again without ever climaxing. Or one of you can have an orgasm and the other not, that's okay too. Honest, there are no rules. So no, I don't think that this is just an elaborate way of kidding ourselves: Rather it's a very simple way to remind ourselves that sexual pleasure can be anything we feel like at a particular time—not just one thing.

This reminder—and the Wednesday-evening picnic—have made a tremendous difference in the sex lives of many couples I know. It has made sex an adventure again, an ongoing experiment. For "Too Busy For Sex" couples, it can be a revelation: Four hours out of one week is really not very much at all—and oh, what a lovely four hours they are. For partners who have resented always making love on the other's schedule, it is a great equalizer: The schedule is set by both of you. And for the Hard Workers and the High Scorers, the leisure and demand-lessness of an evening without bedroom critics to please or batting averages to keep up makes sex a genuine pleasure again rather than a chore.

Some couples ask me, "What if we finish making love at nine o'clock and still have two hours of the evening left to go?"

You might take a little nap or watch a half hour of TV. And you can always go into the kitchen and make more sandwiches. You can talk some more and look some more and touch some more. The idea that orgasm marks the end of all sensual and sexual desire is one of the most absurdly mistaken ideas of all time.

And here's a truly reckless idea for what to do for the rest of the evening: *You can make love again!*

Remember that? How delicious it was? Well, despite popular mythology, "doing it twice" is not just an option for teenagers and sexual athletes. Married folks can do it too. As a matter of fact, I've spoken to a great number of retirees who have suddenly rediscovered this lost art. A middle-aged man may require somewhat longer than a teenager to regain potency after an orgasm, but physically speaking, it need not take that much longer: an hour, maybe two. Nor are you as exhausted as you think you are: For the average man to achieve orgasm requires about the same amount of energy as walking three city blocks. What prevents most couples from "doing it twice" is that they simply never thought they could.

"Can I Have a Glass of Water, Mommy?" and Other Sexual Disasters

There is one final question which always comes up: "What in the world do we tell our friends? And our kids?"

Something very much like the truth. One couple I know simply put out the word: "Wednesdays we always spend home alone together."

Some of their friends leered and winked. And some others seemed genuinely nonplussed, as if the couple had just declared that they had joined a bizarre cult. And there was one friend who was quite worried. "What's the matter? Are you two having problems?" this friend asked.

"No," the couple replied. "We're having fun."

Children present a more pressing problem and not just on "picnic" nights. Time and again couples tell me that it is "impossible" to have sex anymore now that there are children in the house.

It is not impossible; it just requires more planning. *Rule One* of any household with children is *put a lock on the bedroom door and use it.* You are not rejecting your children by doing this; you are simply creating your own privacy. It is far easier to get over your guilt for shutting your children out of your sex lives than it is to get over your resentment toward your children for inhibiting your sex life. By the time your child is two years old it is not too early to begin teaching him or her that there are times when you want to be alone, just as there are times when the child wants to be able to close his or her door and be alone.

Rule Two is *not* to have your only television set in your bedroom. I am constantly amazed by how many couples turn their bedrooms into "family rooms" and then curse the fact that they never have any privacy for sex. Make your bedroom your own private room if you want to enjoy uninhibited, undistracted sex in it.

There are two other solutions to the problem of having uninterrupted sex when there are young children in the house.

First, try "Sexing Out" (see Chapter 14) every once in a while, just as you occasionally dine out leaving the children with a sitter. Another simple solution is to hire a sitter to take the children to the playground or a matinee on a Saturday afternoon so that you can have time and privacy to enjoy sex at home.

Still, with young children at home there will inevitably be the occasional knock on the bedroom door and "Mommy, can I have a glass of water?" right in the middle of lovemaking. Try your best to stay calm and say, "I'll be there in a few minutes, honey." One woman I know felt so "liberated" by just saying this that she immediately went into orgasm.

It also may happen one night that you forget to lock your bedroom door and you will be "caught in the act" by a sleepy little one who wonders what's going on in here. Whatever you do, do not become alarmed or panicked and do not get angry. Only by making the episode into a "big deal" do you risk upsetting the child. Refrain from jumping guiltily out of bed or from trying right then and there to explain the facts of life. Take your time; slowly guide the child back to his own bed and, when you come back, remember this time to lock your door.

Older children present a different problem. If you wait for your teenagers to retire before you start your picnic you may be up all night.

I see nothing in the world wrong with closing *and locking* the bedroom door one evening a week and saying to your older kids, "Your Mom and I want to have some time alone together tonight. Please don't disturb us unless there's a real emergency."

They may giggle. And as they grow older, they just might guess what the two of you are doing behind those doors. And I say "Bravo" to that. Because it will probably be the best—and most reassuring—bit of sexual education they get in their young lives. With any luck, they'll grow up to have marvelous Wednesday-evening picnics of their own.

13
Only When It's Good

When Woody Allen was asked if he thought sex was dirty, the comedian replied, "Only when it's good."

"Dirtiness," "naughtiness," "illicitness"—these have always been part of sexual excitement. But, alas, these elements are usually lost in the seriousness of married sex. When we take our marriage vows, the "Forbidden Game" of sex suddenly becomes the Job of Sex. What was once illicit is now a demand. As one husband said to me, "For the first half of my life, sex was something I wasn't supposed to do and now in the second half it's something I have to do. The first half was certainly a lot more fun."

For most of us, our early sexual experiences were "sneaky" affairs in the backseats of cars, hidden spots in the woods, or in the basement rumpus room. "Breaking the rules" was half the thrill of it all—we were thumbing our noses at society, getting one up on our parents—and that excitement was only intensified by the risk of being caught in the act.

"When I was in high school, I used to take my boyfriend down into the basement playroom," one woman told me. "And every time we heard footsteps upstairs we'd start buttoning up and getting all panicky. But as I look back on it now I realize that was all part of the titillation—buttoning and unbuttoning, holding our breath, all that starting and stopping kept us at a feverish pitch. Who had time to worry about quality of sex? We were too busy just trying to get it done."

For better or for worse, these early "rule breaking" sexual exploits conditioned our experience of sex—the illicitness became part of the package of sex. These early exploits gave us an appetite for a little "naughtiness" in our sex lives.

Some of my colleagues believe that the current "epidemic" of sexual apathy is a direct result of the Sexual Revolution: "With everything allowed, sex lost its illicitness," one colleague said. "And with no rules to break, apathy set in."

Perhaps he is right, but sex has *always* lost its illicitness in marriage and that can be a problem for most of us: *In marriage with no rules to break, apathy can set in.* In fact, I would venture to say that the greatest single cause of marital infidelity is a yearning to "break the rules"—to recapture some of the illicitness and sneakiness which made our original sexual experiences so thrilling. One man I spoke with learned this lesson in a painful way:

"When I was married to Linda, my affair with Sarah was the best sex I ever had," he said. "We'd sneak off to hotel rooms during lunch hour or we'd meet on the sly after work and find some place to make love—my office, the car—any place would do. Later, after I separated and had my own apartment, we'd make love only there, of course, and we didn't have to be sneaky about it either. Somehow, the sex started to drop off almost immediately. It just wasn't as exciting anymore. In about two months, the affair ended. I hate to admit it, but I think we both missed all that danger and sneaking around. Later, it was just like married sex all over again."

I maintain that if we took half the energy we put—or are tempted to put—into affairs and put it instead into making our married sex lives a little "naughtier," we could have our cake and eat it too. We could recapture that thrill of "breaking the rules" without having to break our marriages. All it takes is a little imagination and a little guts.

"Stop right there!" I can hear some of you protesting. *"Just because we learned about sex on the sly, I see no reason why we should cater to our neuroses now. Mature sex doesn't have to be naughty. Anyway, we're too old for games."*

No, mature sex does not *have* to be "naughty," but in most cases that sure goes a long way toward keeping it exciting. The

very notion of "mature sex" sounds rather dull to me: It smacks
of joyless duty totally devoid of any playfulness. And as for
catering to our neuroses, I wonder if that is entirely true: Even
in the most liberated societies, there is something "uncivilized"
about sex—especially *when it is good.* Sex, at its best, brings us
closer to our "animal" selves and further from our "socialized"
selves—it is always a "breaking of the rules" of civilized behavior. Finally, to say you are "too old for games" sounds frighten-
ingly like you think you are "too old for sex" too.

Sexing Out

One couple, Terri and Borden V., told me that the only time
they had any real fun sexually was the two weeks they spent
each summer on Nantucket.

"It's as if we are totally different people the minute we arrive
at the cottage," Borden said. "Usually, as soon as the kids go off
to the beach, we get undressed and go at it right then and there.
It's marvelous."

"But two weeks isn't a hell of a lot," Terri chimed in. "I start
counting the days the minute we come home again."

Most couples enjoy more active sex lives on their vacations.
They have left the anxieties of work and running a home behind
them; they can break out of the inhibiting routines and dulling
habits associated with home and bedroom; they are more
rested, more relaxed, happier. All of these factors contribute to
a better atmosphere for sex. But there is another factor: Making
love in a different place—in a different bed—and doing it at
different times of day and night—recaptures some of the adventure of "naughty sex." In the case of Terri and Borden, not only
did they make love more frequently during their two-week
holiday, but they tried variations which they somehow never
got around to trying at home. In short, they "broke all the
rules."

The advice I gave to them is advice which I think could spice
up the sex lives of just about every couple—take "Evening
Vacations." "Sex Out" as often as you can:

Instead of getting a sitter and *dining out* or going out to the movies or theater, get a sitter and go out for an evening of sex in a hotel or motel. When you add it up, the cost is almost the same. And it can be infinitely more fun.

There is no need to limit "vacation sex" to two weeks a year— you can have it once a week or fortnightly.

"Sexing Out" helps us get out from under the "demand" of sex. It makes it a treat instead of a duty. We go out for the explicit purpose of having sexual fun instead of staying home and putting in a routine performance. Just this simple change in routine made a world of difference for Terri and Borden. Terri said:

"The first night when we registered at the Holiday Inn without any luggage, the clerk gave us this suspicious, disapproving look and it was all we could do to keep from giggling until we were alone in the room. We started this joke that the house detective was going to break down the door and demand to see our marriage license. Half the time we laughed and the other half we made love. When we got home, the sitter asked if we had enjoyed the movie and we started giggling all over again. Next time, we went to a motel over in Jersey and Borden registered us as George and Martha Washington. This time, the clerk winked. We had a marvelous time again."

As Terri and Borden made "Sexing Out" part of their lives, their sex at home improved too, becoming more frequent *and* more various: "It was sort of a trickle-down effect," Borden said. "We brought some of the 'motel' home with us."

A little "naughtiness" can go a long way. Other couples I know not only "Sex Out" from time to time, but they seek out novel settings every time. One woman told me, "One night we'll 'Sex Out' in a fancy hotel and next time we'll find the raunchiest, fleabag hotel. Once, we found a sort of old-world rooming house in a town not far from ours; it was the perfect setting for a 'secret affair'—straight out of *Betrayal* or something. Strange as it sounds, it became a whole fantasy for us—we were having this 'secret affair' *with each other.*"

It did not sound strange to me at all. A new setting frequently unleashes exciting fantasies for us. It frees us to be "someone else" for a little while, to be Mystery Lovers.

"For a change, I saw Myra as my lover instead of just my wife," one man told me. "She even *looked* different when I got her in a different bed. Somewhere along the line we even adopted nicknames for each other which we use only when we are in hotel rooms."

Another couple I know—a usually very prim and proper pair —like to "Sex Out" from time to time in X-Rated motels: Motels equipped with pornographic videos and overhead mirrors.

"It's our secret," the wife told me. "None of our friends know about it. We just go crazy and raunchy every few weeks. We'd probably be terribly embarrassed if anyone found out, but I don't think that's the only reason we don't tell anyone—it's also because it makes it more exciting to have a 'secret life.' "

This particular couple were terribly inhibited with their sex at home and that never completely changed—there was no "trickle-down effect" for them. Yet they had found a perfectly harmless and exciting way to keep their sex lives from disappearing altogether. "Sexing Out" was not only the best sex they had, it was virtually the only sex they had. But it was infinitely better than no sex at all.

There is one other couple whose "Sexing Out" adventures I want to mention because they found extra excitement in "breaking old rules." They found that every time they spent a weekend with her parents they were up half the night making love.

"At first we didn't realize why this happened every time," the wife told me. "And then one night when we heard my parents coming up the stairs after we were already in bed we realized what the 'turn-on' was all about. It made us feel silly and a little ashamed to realize that we were getting off on being 'bad little children.' But after a while we decided, 'What the heck! It's fun!' We go over there about one weekend a month now and we have great sex every time."

The more power to them, I say.

Write Your Own X-Rated Movies

Without some element of fantasy, sex can become a pretty prosaic business. As one man I know jokingly put it, "Fantasy in sex is what separates us from the animals. Any pair of dogs can copulate, but only Man can make it into a production."

The best "productions" I hear about usually have an X-Rated quality to them—they are shared fantasies about "breaking the rules."

Several couples I know who "Sex Out" like to fantasize that they are having an extramarital affair. Some heighten this fantasy by arriving at the hotel separately and others like to set up their "assignations" at the last minute to make it more of an adventure.

"Sometimes my husband calls me at my office," one woman told me, "and all he says is, 'The Lexington Hotel at five o'clock.' I get goose bumps when he does that."

Another couple told me that they play the "affair" game at home.

"Once, in the middle of everything, my wife suddenly said, 'Hurry, my husband's coming.' It was both funny and wonderful at the same time. Sometimes she even complains to me about her 'husband' and I can take it all in without getting uptight. I'm the sympathetic lover and it's amazing how understanding I can be of her 'husband's' faults."

Frequently, after telling me about their fantasy games, couples tell me that they feel somewhat guilty and ashamed for playing them.

"I feel like I'm cheating by pretending so much of the time," one woman told me. "It doesn't feel right not to be myself when we are having sex."

And one man said, "I hate to think that the games and fantasies we use are a crutch we need to have good sex. It makes me think there is something abnormal about us."

To each of these couples I say, you're lucky that you can enjoy your fantasies. They're a terrific break from all the routines of daily life. No one is really cheated: You are playing these games *together*. And part of the thrill of sexual fantasies is that you have double vision: You are yourself *and* somebody else at the same time. No, there is nothing abnormal about sexual fantasies. It is just that some of us are more explicit about them and better at them than others. (Interestingly, I have had some people come to me recently who are worried because they do *not* have sexual fantasies. To them also, I say, "If your sex is good, what is there to worry about?")

I know several people for whom playing out sexual fantasies has made all the difference between satisfying and unsatisfying sex lives. One woman I know was nonorgasmic until she and her husband started playing the "naughty" game of pretending that she was a prostitute: "Afterwards, I'd always say, 'Just leave your money on the dresser.' There is just something about this game which frees me up—my husband too. I suppose it's 'perverted' but I have orgasms all the time now."

By playing "whore," this woman was able to let go of all the "good girl" inhibitions which were preventing her from enjoying herself. The fantasy was a shortcut which worked. Her husband enjoyed it too—no harm done to anyone. I would be the last one to call that perverse.

I am frequently asked if sexual aids such as pornographic pictures, books, and videos, and vibrators and other paraphernalia can help a couple "spice up" a flagging sex life. The answer, like that to so many sexual questions, is: "They can if you want them to. And if neither of you is upset by them."

Many people—especially women—find pornography demeaning; in particular they find it demeaning to the women who pose for it. Obviously, if either of you take this moral position, pornography is not right for you. For some women, pornographic pictures may also raise a jealousy issue. They do not enjoy the idea of their partner's thinking about the body of the woman in the *Penthouse* centerfold (often a younger body than their own) while they are having sex together. Again, this is a case where pornography is not right for you. But if you are not upset by it, and a picture, movie, or raunchy passage of a book helps set off a sexual fantasy for you both, I certainly see no harm in using it to get aroused or to get new sexual "ideas."

Many couples I know use X-Rated videos on their home viewers as a prelude to sex. The fact is, they are the best-selling cassettes in America.

"We'd never be caught dead in some raunchy movie house," one husband told me, "but with a cassette, we can wait until the kids are asleep and have our own private viewing. The first time I brought a film home my wife was a little put off by the idea. But when we ended up making love on the floor before it was half over, she decided it wasn't such a bad idea after all. The whole thing—floor and all—made us feel like horny teenagers."

Another couple told me that after a while they became "connoisseurs" of dirty movies:

"We kept saying, 'If I had directed this movie, I would have had them do this or that instead.' After a while, we were writing our own X-Rated movies right there in front of the TV—and acting them out, of course. We did things we never thought of trying before, while the 'cameras' were capturing it all. I have to admit, our sex life has gotten better since we became our own 'porn' stars."

Again, here was a couple who found a sexual fantasy which worked for both of them, allowing them both to be freer and more adventurous by putting some naughtiness into their sex lives. But like many other such couples, they were worried that they would become dependent on their little game.

"What could be better than being dependent on your own imaginations?" I asked them. In effect, they were asking my permission to be bad. But they did not need that—being "bad" never requires permission.

By the same token, vibrators and other paraphernalia sold in sex shops can add variety to your sex life if used hygienically and *if neither of you is offended by them.* But if your partner finds such aids degrading or frightening, nothing can be gained by browbeating or guilt-tripping him or her into trying them; *that* can end all sex.

How to Talk Dirty and Influence People

One couple who came to me complaining that they did not have the "time for sex" were actually telling the truth. They were each in a profession which required frequent extended business trips away from home. Often, they were home together only one out of every four weeks.

"Neither of us wants to have affairs," the husband told me, "but masturbating alone in a hotel room can be a pretty lonely business. We've thought of quitting or changing our jobs. We've even discussed divorce—but that's not what either of us wants."

"Why not have sex over the phone?" I asked them. "It is certainly better than nothing."

As it turned out, "Phone Sex" was a *lot better* than nothing for these two. Over the months, they refined it into a very sexy art. The woman told me, "Usually, we begin by taking turns telling each other what we would do to each other if we were together. What we would touch and how, then what we'd do next. It's amazing how much detail we go into. Then, when we're good and aroused, we talk about what we are doing to ourselves and how it feels. We make a lot of noise into the phone when we come. It's terrific."

Her husband added that their Phone Sex had enlivened their one week a month together immeasurably: "It's like we're picking up where we left off in our last conversation instead of having to get sexually reacquainted all over again. Before, it took us half the week just to do that. But besides that, there's something about the Phone Sex which gets both of our imaginations going. We talk about doing things to each other which we never tried before. But now when we get together, we do try them."

Sexy phone conversations allowed this couple's sexual imaginations to soar as they never had before. Surely, the real distance between them allowed them to do this by removing the anxieties which would have been present if they had been in the same room. But, as the woman realized, there was something else at play here too. "Let's face it," she said, "we're making obscene phone calls to each other. We even breathe hard. It makes me feel wonderfully 'naughty'—especially after a long day of meetings in my 'Miss Prim' business suit."

I often encourage couples who complain of humdrum sex lives to try talking dirty with each other, either over the phone or in person. Over the phone, as we have seen, can be the best way to start because it is less threatening. One woman told me that she and her husband made frequent "quickie, obscene phone calls" to each other all day: "I get him on the phone— even if he is in the middle of a meeting—and I'll say something like 'Don't move—I just stuck my hand in your fly. Talk to you later.' We have a good laugh, but there's no denying that it's a real turn-on."

Another couple I know who were perpetually turned off by the interruptions and general inhibitions of home life—they had four children at home—instituted the ritual of whispering "dirty nothings" into each other's ears when they greeted each other in the evenings.

"Instead of the old sexless peck on the cheek while the kids tug at us," the wife told me, "we give each other a hug and whisper the most scandalous things into each other's ears— *while the kids are tugging at us.* Still, it seems to carry over until we're at last alone. By that time we're ready to suit actions to words."

"Talking dirty" changed the whole way they saw one another. Instead of being suffocated by the sexless atmosphere of a busy home, they "broke the rules" and whispered "scandalous things" to one another right there in front of the unhearing children. Instead of being overwhelmed by a sexless setting, they used the setting to be "naughty."

"Talk Me into It"

Time and again, men and women tell me that what they miss most in married sex is the titillation of *seduction.* One woman, Liz Q., told me, "Before we were married, Hal always made a

big production out of getting me into bed. It started with flowers, went on to wine and soft music and romantic talk, and then
he'd kiss me and talk some more before he went on. It was
lovely. *And now it's all gone!* Now, he waits until bedtime and
then he wants to go at it the minute he gets into bed."

This was a woman who found that she was rarely "in the
mood" for sex with her husband anymore. She had concocted a
whole litany of excuses—from headaches to menstrual pains—
for refusing his late-night, perfunctory advances. As far as Liz
was concerned, her married sex was just a duty now, nothing
more; the thrill was definitely gone.

"Next time he wants to make love without any preliminar-
ies," I told her, "instead of saying you have a headache, say to
him, 'Talk me into it.' Perhaps you can put some seduction back
into your sex life."

I went on to say that if she tried this "game," she had to be
willing to be willing to have sex. In other words, she did not
have to promise that she would be "talked into sex," but she had
to at least open the door to that possibility.

An occasional game of "Talk Me into It" is an exciting way for
most of us to break out of the lazy routines of "Let's Get It Out
of the Way" married sex. For performance-oriented men in
particular, it can bring back the thrill of conquest: The wife is
not just lying there awaiting—nay, *demanding*—her "quota" of
sex, she has to be "made." The husband has to be seductive
enough—i.e., perform well enough—to "score." Likewise, for
women (in particular) who miss the "romance" of seduction, the
flattering attention and dreamy mood of being courted by an
ardent lover can make her feel more desirable—and hence,
more sexual. As well, for many women such as Liz, asking the
husband to "Talk Me into It" helps them to break out of the
cycle of "sexual sacrifice." Instead of always "giving in" to sex as
one more marital duty, the woman can play out the age-old
feminine fantasy of having her lover "pay for" her sexual favors
with flowers and assurances of love. For both the man and the
woman in this scenario, the game of seduction draws out the
sexual encounter, makes it less rushed, more gradually titillating—just as sex used to be before we compressed it all to a
purely genital act. And there is another element from our ear-

lier sexual experiences which "Talk Me into It" can reignite: *the sexual tension of not knowing how it will turn out.* Will she or won't she? Instead of the foregone conclusion that married sex so often becomes, the titillating game goes on anew. Knowing that sex is a fait accompli before we even begin can make us rush to the end; but not knowing how it will turn out makes it an adventure every moment along the way.

But there are dangers in this game too. The first time that Liz asked her husband, Hal, to "Talk Me into It," his response was "You must be kidding!" As far as he was concerned, now that they were married, "games" were out of the question. In my office, he said, "It's ridiculous to have to seduce my own wife. That part of our life is over now. We aren't teenagers anymore."

"Do you mean that sex should not be playful anymore now that you are married?" I asked him.

He shrugged. "I mean that I don't have the time for all that rigamarole at this point in my life. I work hard all day; I don't want to have to work hard to get some sexual release in my own home."

Hal, apparently, had enough time for sex; he just did not have "enough time" to make it an exciting experience for both of them. He saw seduction as work rather than as pleasure.

"Which is better?" I asked him. "Your wife's 'headaches' or a sexual adventure which takes a little energy and initiative on your part?"

Again, he shrugged, but the next time Liz asked him to "Talk Me into It" he made a little effort to "seduce" her.

"*Very* little effort," Liz told me later. "He ran his hand through my hair and said something about how nice I looked and that was it. He wanted to get started right then and there. I just couldn't get in the mood. And he got good and mad. He said he had tried my little game and if that wasn't enough to forget it."

"Let's start all over again," I told her, "but this time *you seduce him.* And get started early in the evening before he even gives a thought to sex."

Liz resisted. She said it just made sex "all for him" again, but I convinced her that it was worth a try. It was. In my office, even Hal admitted that it had been fun: "It was a real game of cat and mouse. She'd say something provocative and then when I'd reach out for her, she'd skitter away into the other room, then come back in and unbutton my shirt and rub my chest. It went on for hours."

For Hal, it suddenly was not so bad to play games. Without realizing it, he had grown tired of his role of "sexual initiator," which had begun even before he married Liz. That, in part, accounted for his sexual "laziness," and it clearly accounted for his resistance to playing "Talk Me into It." For once, he wanted to be talked into it. When I suggested that they *take turns* playing the game, he was much more willing. He talked her into it the next time and they both agreed it was a marvelous evening. After a while, the game of "Talk Me into It" became the game of "Who's Going to Seduce Whom Tonight?"—a game which proved even more exciting for both of them.

The First Time—Again

In every seduction, there is an element of "naughtiness." The tension and suspense of "will she or won't she?" makes it a forbidden game, a breaking down of rules. And this element can be intensified by changing the setting of the seduction from the bedroom at home to the scene of our early seductions—the car, the drive-in, a restaurant, or motel. It is all part of recapturing the feeling of the way we made love before routines and foregone conclusions robbed it of its spontaneity.

Whenever a married couple tells me that their sex life has lost its pizzazz, I tell them to try to recall a specific sexual experience they had together in the past when it was still exciting. Just about everyone has at least one such experience he can remember.

"We were at a movie," one woman told me, "a ridiculous comedy that neither of us was particularly interested in. And we started to make out. What a wonderful term that is—'making out'—I'd almost forgotten it. Well, we really went at it hot and heavy. My bra was undone, my hand was on his crotch. At one point we just looked at each other and rushed out to the car and made love right there in the parking lot. It was fantastic! But I guess it's a hard act to follow: We never have."

"Do it 'the first time' again," I told her and her husband. "Go to a movie—the more boring the better—and 'make out.' Go as far as you can. Break all the rules."

It is an experiment we all could enjoy:

Pick out the setting of a hot sexual experience you had in the past—a bus, a car, a porch swing, whatever. And then make out and pet as you did then.

One couple I know occasionally go out to their car in the driveway at night and "make out" like teenagers.

"Sure, it's crazy," the husband said, "but it's fun. When I think back on it, 'making out' was more exciting back then than the one-two-three sex we have in our bedroom. Now we pet in the car and race inside to the bedroom. It's the best of both worlds."

In most marriages, "petting"—especially while we are still dressed or partially dressed—is only a fond memory. It seems absurd to bother with it when we know that we can just get undressed and go to bed if we want to. But that "bother" was once thrilling. Why should we lose it just because everything is permitted? Yet to break out of the "one-two-three sex" pattern at home is too difficult for most of us. We have to change our mind-set and there is no better way than by changing our setting.

"At first, we felt too self-conscious to get started when we tried to re-create the first time we had great sex," one woman told me. "We had gone to the same motel, even the same room, and we just stood around looking at each other like we were strangers. But eventually that turned out to be what made it so good. It was as if we were as shy with each other as we had been way back then. It was really very romantic and moving. We go back to that motel every month or so. We must have done it 'the first time' about twenty times by now."

Going Public—the Naughtiest Sex There Is

The couple who "made out" in their driveway admitted to me that part of the thrill for them was the effect it had on the neighbors.

"Occasionally we'll see the lady next door peering out at us from behind the curtains," the husband said, "and we'll duck down behind the seat and giggle away and go at it some more. We're sure she's jealous of us."

Basic to all "naughtiness" in sex is the element of thumbing our nose at the rest of the world. Breaking rules, after all, is a social act: We cannot be "bad" or "dirty" unless there is a society out there to disapprove . . . and to threaten to "catch us" at it. For many of us, the "naughtiest" and most thrilling sex there is, is sex which flirts with public discovery.

"*Stop right there!*" (That voice of protest, louder than ever.) "*If you are going to recommend exhibitionism for the sake of a 'cheap thrill,' I've had enough of your 'healthy' advice. What two people do alone is their business, but what they do in public is everybody's business. And what you are recommending is a disgusting business.*"

First, I would never recommend exhibitionism to anybody. Among other things, public nudity and public sex are against the law. But what I do recommend to those who, like Woody Allen, think that sex is dirty "only when it's good" is that they experiment with sex which treads *close to the edge* of public view. We will still be doing it alone. No one needs to be harmed or scandalized. Yet we will recapture some of the thrill of breaking the rules.

For some of us, the very idea of "going public" fills us with anxiety. There are those of us who still are not comfortable with the tamest of public affection—who cannot even stop and kiss on a street corner without being overcome by embarrassment and shame. And *that* is a shame: A public kiss has a tingle all of its own—a very sexy tingle. It is a good place to start:

Next time you two are alone in the street on the way to a show or dinner, stop and kiss each other right there.

Don't worry, you won't get arrested. You may hear a few giggles, but mostly you will probably just get envious looks.

"Affection is private," I hear that voice protesting again. *"And being affectionate in public cheapens it."*

If you think that public affection cheapens it, then, of course, it does. But that is *your* opinion, not everyone's—and not mine. For me, when I see a couple embrace or kiss in public, I find I like the world a little bit more. It can put me in a romantic mood for hours.

But it is where public affection merges with public sex that things get tricky. And can get very exciting. Again, start with something tame:

Next time you kiss in public, whisper something "dirty" in each other's ears. Again, no harm is done—no one will be arrested or scandalized. But your "dirty little secret" may start you tingling for the rest of the day.

Public "dirty secrets" can be terrific fun. Whenever they go to a party, one couple I know occasionally sidle up to one another and whisper lascivious messages in each other's ears before drifting away to the party again.

"Our friends always ask us what the big secret is," the woman told me. "We tell them we're working for the CIA."

It is the secretiveness which makes these public games exciting and which, in a way, can make us feel closer to one another: The secret is ours and no one else's. But, of course, we cannot enjoy the thrill of secretiveness in our own bedrooms at eleven o'clock—there is absolutely nothing "sneaky" about that.

When I was a student at the Karolinska Institute in Stockholm, we had the choice of two elevators: one with a window, the other without. Couples almost invariably chose the windowless elevator: It provided a private-but-almost-public setting for some quick "making out" between classes. The game, of course, was to see how far you could go before the doors slid open again.

Not every couple made the deadline. And that is what made the game exciting.

Probably all of us have fantasies about having sex in public. Certainly, the media have picked up on the popularity of this fantasy: The best remembered scene from the movie *Shampoo* depicts Julie Christie crawling under the table at a formal dinner party and, hidden by the tablecloth, attempting to have oral sex with Warren Beatty. Much of the titillation of this scene comes from the fact that it is a *formal* party; the idea would not have been half as exciting if they had been at a dark and sleazy nightclub. No one I know would dare to go as far as the Julie Christie character did in that film, but there are public games which we can enjoy which are not quite so daring.

One woman told me that she and her husband love going out to fancy restaurants and "doing naughty things" under the table.

"Somewhere around the soup course, I slip off my shoe and place my stockinged foot squarely in his crotch and kind of gently move it around. It drives him crazy. I've found that you can get away with anything if you are dressed like a 'lady.' "

Playing the role of a "lady" or "gentleman" is part of the fun —we are turned on by the contrast of all this civilized formality with the "naughty things" we are doing in secret.

Another couple I know occasionally go into a hotel lobby phone booth together and—she on his lap—do "all kinds of naughty things" to each other just hidden from view while one of them pantomimes making a phone call.

"Sometimes we'll even make a real phone call," the husband said, "and carry on a conversation while we're grabbing each other. I wouldn't recommend it for important business calls, though."

Taking their cue from the film *Emmanuelle,* another couple I know like to sneak off to the public lavatory when they are on airplanes and make love behind the locked door. Public transportation seems to offer all kinds of opportunities for public-but-hidden sex: Another couple told me that they wait until the in-flight movie goes on, spread a blanket over both their laps and play with each other under it. No harm is done; no one ever knows—but the thrill of treading close to that boundary is very much there.

Make a Joyful Noise

Inhibitions are like a string of firecrackers: When we "explode" one—break through it—several other inhibitions can explode automatically, freeing us to enjoy sex more fully. But the reverse is also true: When we inhibit one aspect of our sexuality, we automatically inhibit several aspects, making sex nervous and less than satisfactory. One little explosion that can set off marvelous sexual fireworks is allowing ourselves to be noisy in sex. It is against the "rules"—it treads close to public sex —but that, of course, is what makes it so much fun.

"Make a Joyful Noise" is an exercise I recommend to every couple. Not only does it promote that thrill of illicitness, but it is a release in itself—a "letting go" which makes all our sexual feelings more explosive. But for many of us, it means breaking through a very substantial inhibition.

First and foremost, we are afraid of what the children or neighbors will think if we moan and yell too loudly or if we laugh too raucously. But usually, this is an exaggerated fear: Our television sets and stereos are probably just as loud as the noises we will make—the children will undoubtedly sleep through our noises. And furthermore, we can leave the stereo on to cover our sounds. One couple told me that they put on the *1812 Overture* whenever they make love: "Anyone who hears us through all those drums and cannons must be lying under our bed."

As it turns out, our real fear about making noise is what each of us will think. Many women have told me that they are afraid to make anything more than a little whimper when they reach orgasm because they do not want to "sound like some slut." A moan or scream or throaty laugh is too "unladylike" for them: "Good girls" only make "good girl" sounds.

To these women I say, "A 'good girl' usually doesn't have much fun in bed. And a good way to stop being a 'good girl' and start having more fun is by opening your mouth and screaming with pleasure."

But, very often, it is their husbands they are worried about—what will they think? True, some men who are stuck on the idea that wives are "madonnas" will be put off by a good moan; yet often, it can help them break out of this sex-dulling mind-set. In spite of themselves, they find that noisy sex turns them on; they see that their wives are truly sexual beings for the first time and they realize they can have some "dirty" fun at home, not just in their fantasies or with "low" women. There are also men who are threatened by a vocally responsive wife because they hear her moans and screams as a demand: How can they ever "perform" well enough to equal her response? But again, by gradually getting used to a little "joyful noise," they can become desensitized to this seeming threat and begin to hear their wife's moans and screams as expressions of pleasure—appreciation, in fact—not as a demand. There are women, too, who are initially put off by their husband's grunts and groans during sex; they find it overwhelming, as if they are in bed "with some animal."

"All the better," I tell them. "There is no better place to feel like an animal than in bed."

For many men and women, keeping a "tight lip" during sex is a habit left over from their early experiences with "sneaky" sex —masturbating in the bathroom; petting on the front porch. Too much noise risked discovery then. Yet it is precisely breaking this habit—breaking the rules—which can make noisy sex so exhilarating.

"Making a Joyful Noise" is something we can work up to. Some couples try it first when they are "Sexing Out."

"We were in a motel and I didn't give a hoot who heard us," one woman told me, "so I just opened my mouth and let it all come out. Bill too. We sounded like a regular barnyard in there and after a while we both started laughing."

Gradually, this couple was able to bring their "barnyard" home with them and, like a string of firecrackers, all of their sex became freer: "Somehow when I moan I move differently," the woman told me. "And anything I feel like doing seems game."

Another way to work up to noisy sex is to start by making sexual sounds together totally apart from sexual contact:

Fully dressed but alone together where no one can hear, take turns imitating sexual noises. Be as loud or silly as you want. Make the noises more and more lascivious with each turn until you are both simulating the very noisiest orgasms you can. Don't worry about who will hear you. And don't be afraid to laugh. It's just a game.

But it is a game which can very quickly put us at ease with sexual noises. One couple told me that they went immediately from making "practice" sexual noises to getting undressed and groaning and moaning for real.

"We were surprised how much it turned us on," they said.

It was no surprise to me. They were turning themselves on.

With "joyful noises," as with all the "naughty" exercises we have talked about, we have to approach them gingerly—a little at a time so that neither partner becomes overwhelmed and has to go back to square one. We have to find the level of "naughtiness" with which we are both comfortable; to try to force our partners further risks even more inhibition, not less. But on the other hand, we both have to be willing to be sexually daring and creative: to make up our own exercises and to try them in the spirit of playfulness and adventure. We all have the capacity for that.

Probably the most exhilarating way to be "naughty" is to break the biggest rule of all in married sex—the rule that we should only do the "Real Thing"—sexual intercourse—and nothing else. In the next chapter, Sexual Smorgasbord, we will explore these sexual options. It will take quite a bit of daring for many of us—but perhaps some Joyful Noises can explode the inhibitions and take us there.

14
Sexual Smorgasbord

"Our sex life has become so routine—so boring and predictable —that all I can think about is making it with somebody else."

I cannot begin to count the number of times I have heard this complaint from frustrated men and women who come to see me. And each time I hear them say it, I am struck by the sad, unimaginative ways we limit ourselves: *Most of these people would rather contemplate changing partners than changing their sexual routines with the same partner.*

Habits die hard. We become so locked into our old partner systems of having sex in a particular order and in a particular way that the very thought of breaking out of our sexual routine seems harder and more complicated than, say, changing diets or moving to a new town—or, Heaven help us, changing families. Over the years of making love to the same person we tend to find one way of doing things, a routine that "works," and so we stay with it until that seemingly inevitable day when sexual apathy and boredom set in. In fact, in my experience the people who are *least willing* to try sexual variations—to sample the Sexual Smorgasbord which is available to us all—are those people who never experienced a sexual problem until the day they discovered that they were bored. Those with a specific sexual problem will experiment with most anything to improve their sex lives; but those who have been functioning normally in a narrow sphere of sexual routines do not realize that they have a real problem which has led them down the path of sexual apathy. Their problem is *sexual inflexibility*.

In the "Real Thing" we examined the basic cause of most of this inflexibility. We become stuck with sexual intercourse as the only legitimate and "decent" form of sexual activity for "mature" adults—especially married, mature adults—and thus we dismiss all other sexual variations as inferior forms of sex—childish, dirty, perverse, and demeaning. Even many people who do occasionally try mutual masturbation or oral sex admit that they come away from the experience with a vague sense of discomfort and guilt.

But that is precisely how we can become bored.

I do not urge the sexual variations which follow in this chapter on every couple—I don't want to set up more competitive goals which can make us all feel we are losing the Sexual Sweepstakes. But on the other hand, I do urge every couple to *at least consider* these variations as alternatives to what they are doing now—especially if they feel shortchanged by what they are doing now. Do these variations speak to some secret fantasy you have kept to yourself over the years? Do they seem tempting to try—perhaps just once? We have nothing to lose by simply thinking about these alternatives and by talking about them with each other. And what we have to gain is a whole spectrum of sexual delights, an exciting expansion of our sexual tastes, an array of sexual options which can keep us far from the clutches of sexual boredom.

But even just the talking does not come easily. After all those years it is not easy to blurt out your secret fantasy—to say, in effect, what is missing in your sex life; to say, for example, "I'd really like to try oral sex" after not having done it for fifteen years.

The first rule regarding such conversations is *not* to have them in bed—especially not just before you are about to have sex. It can ruin a perfectly nice evening with guilt and recriminations or worse, fights. The best solution to where and when to talk about "trying something different" was offered to me by one couple who said they met occasionally after work in a cafe to talk about what variation they wanted to try next time they made love.

"Somehow being in a 'neutral zone' made all the difference," the woman told me. "All the pressure and anxiety were off. He'd say, 'Sometimes I wish you'd lick me all over,' and I'd say, 'Me too. Pass the sugar,' and we'd have a good laugh. But next time we had sex, we wouldn't forget what we'd talked about over coffee."

All right, the coffee klatch is over. Now for the Smorgasbord.

Keep Your Pants On

The last time most couples initiated sex with their clothes on was when they were teenagers—probably in the backseat of a car. Once we are grown up and married, however, we usually "get ready," i.e., take our clothes off, before we even begin. What a shame, especially considering how tantalizing it was to press a hand against a covered breast or, locked in an embrace, to thrust our pelvises forward and rub against one another— with our pants on. "Dry humping" used to drive us wild. And working a hand inside a blouse and bra or up a stockinged leg or slipping fingers over a bulging fly was sheer heaven. It *promised* so much to come. Why do we skip these marvelous steps now? Is it so urgent to "get down to business" right away?

"But once you're married, you don't *have to* go through all that rigamarole anymore," people tell me. "You're just drawing things out in an unnecessary teenage game. And you know you're just kidding yourself."

"Fine," I say. "There's nothing wrong with kidding yourself and each other a little bit if it makes for better sex."

The more playfully we work up to sex, the longer we take to "get down to business," the better the sex we are likely to have. Specifically, we are likely to have better orgasms with a longer buildup because there is greater congestion in our sex organs and hence greater release when we finally come.

As well, starting sex play with our clothes on gives us a chance to recapture the thrill of seductive games. Instead of beginning sex in the middle of the game, with its outcome a foregone conclusion, we can play with the almost but not quite qualities of clothes-on sex. We can tease ourselves and each other with the anticipation of "more to come" and wondering "Will she/he or won't she/he?"

Many men and some women enjoy an occasional "surprise grab." For example, in a dark movie theater or sitting on a sofa in front of the TV, you suddenly drop your hand into his lap and give his penis a playful squeeze or he comes up behind you while you are combing your hair and gives your covered breasts a merry tweak. It can either be the beginning of sex which goes "all the way" or it can simply be a little bit of fun—the kind of fun which keeps us feeling sexy and sexual in a marriage. One warning, however: Some men—and many women—do not enjoy a surprise grab. It makes them feel they are being assaulted and they tighten up in a fear response; it may even call up unhappy experiences from the past. In such cases, this is one game which is better left alone.

A harmless game which also seems to get lost in the "down to business" attitude of "grown-up" sex is seductively undressing each other. Indeed, undressing each other before sex seems to have become a lost art. But women, especially, miss the tantalizing excitement of their partner unpinning their hair, slowly unbuttoning their blouses, unzipping their skirts, all the while touching and fondling them. For some, the most erotic touching comes during this process. One sexually happy woman told me, "My husband can sometimes take a whole half hour undressing me. And he always leaves my undies on until the very end, pressing and caressing my vagina through the silk. Sometimes I come before my pants are even off."

This woman wanted to know if there was anything "abnormal" about their sex life.

"You aren't abnormal," I told her. "You're just lucky."

Hands-On Sex

Masturbation has had a bad name ever since we were children. "Self-abuse" it was called, and along with being told that it would cause warts on our hands or stunt our growth, we were warned that it could become addictive—like drugs or cigarettes —which would prevent us from enjoying the "Real Thing" once we grew up. Indeed, adult masturbation is still seen as regressive and any adult who persists in this "depraved" practice must be ugly, old, or weird, someone who is incapable of finding a sexual partner. Many people have told me with more than a touch of pride that once they got married they "gave up" masturbation as if they were telling me that they had given up whisky. Yet in fact, the great majority of adults do masturbate, alone and secretively and usually somewhat shamefully. Bringing masturbation out of the closet and into the bed you share with your mate takes courage. But it is courage which can pay off in a more thrilling and varied sex life.

First and foremost, sharing masturbation provides both of you with an exciting alternative to the "Real Thing." It allows you to make other sexual practices pleasurable *in themselves*, not just as warm-ups to sexual intercourse. And, once you are both comfortable with it, sharing masturbation permits some of the joys of regression, calling up those exciting memories of furtive teenage sex when the "Real Thing" was either not allowed or there was no place to do it.

At a fundamental emotional level, sharing masturbation with your partner provides an unusual opportunity for closeness: By sharing your "shameful" secret with each other, you share your vulnerabilities with each other—and what a joyful relief that can be. But it can be tricky: By masturbating yourself in front of each other (what I call "tandem" masturbation) or by masturbating each other (mutual masturbation), you are admitting that you sometimes masturbate in private, that sex with your partner is not the only sex you indulge in. Some partners may automatically see this as a form of rejection at first—that is, until they admit to themselves that when they masturbate it has nothing at all to do with rejection. For men who are stuck with an image of their wives as "madonnas" without sexual needs or desires of their own, shared masturbation can remove their wives from their pedestals and allow them to be seen as real sexual beings with whom they can enjoy all kinds of sexual variations—not just the "Real Thing."

Alternate masturbation (either doing it yourself in front of